First published in 2012
by Franklin Watts

Text © Roy Apps 2012
Illustrations by Ollie Cuthbertson © Franklin Watts 2012
Cover design by Jonathan Hair
and Peter Scoulding

Franklin Watts
338 Euston Road
London NW1 3BH

Franklin Watts Australia
Level 17/207 Kent Street
Sydney, NSW 2000

A CIP catalogue record for this book
is available from the British Library.

ISBN: 978 1 4451 0336 5

1   3   5   7   9   10   8   6   4   2

Printed in Great Britain

Franklin Watts is a division of Hachette Children's Books,
an Hachette UK company.
www.hachette.co.uk

CONTENTS

Don't Look Behind You

The Babysitter

Don't Look Behind You

~1~

Suddenly he felt very alone...

Harjit had always liked cars.

He'd passed his driving test first time, just a month after his seventeenth birthday. He had used all the money he had saved from his weekend job at the supermarket to buy a cheap Fiat Punto. He'd customised it; added racing seats and a top of the range music system.

Tonight was the first time Harjit had actually driven alone. He'd met a couple of his mates in Welton, where they had gone bowling at the new leisure complex. Afterwards he'd offered to give them both a lift home. Well, it was freezing outside.

But even if it had been a warm summer's night, Harjit would still have offered to give them a lift: he wanted to show off his new car.

Harjit and his family lived about ten miles away, on the outskirts of a neighbouring town. His mate Paul lived close to the town centre, so Harjit dropped him off first. Then he took Aaron out to his place on the big estate up on the hill. Harjit stayed, listening to some new tracks Aaron had downloaded.

It was late when Harjit left, and thick, icy rain had started to beat down heavily. He ran to the car, the rain stinging his face. He zapped the doors with his key, eager to get inside the car and out of the rain. Suddenly, he heard a voice shout out. It was Aaron. "Harj! You've forgotten your cap!"

Aaron stood on the doorstep waving Harjit's baseball cap in his hand. Harjit turned and ran back up the path to get it.

Just as he got back to the car, he thought he heard a voice behind him in the dark: an urgent, desperate voice that seems to hiss at him through the rain. "Psst! Over here!" Harjit swung round. Aaron had gone back inside. It was the wind playing tricks, Harjit thought, and with that he jumped into his car and pulled the door shut.

Harjit sank into the moulded leather racing seat and started the engine. He stabbed the button for his favourite local station and turned up the volume.

As he swung the car out of the estate and onto the main road, Harjit glanced in the rear-view mirror and saw a pair of headlights close behind him. Not modern halogen or LED lights, but the old-fashioned kind; large, round and yellowy.

Harjit left the glow of the town streetlamps behind him and headed out into the countryside. The windscreen wipers thrashed at the rain. Shadows of the hedgerows and bare trees loomed up on each side of the car like deformed monster shapes. Music thumped in his ears. Harjit checked the rear-view mirror. The round, yellow headlights were still there.

Suddenly Harjit felt very alone.

2

This man is extremely violent!

Another quick glance in his rear-view mirror and Harjit saw the car behind him swerve out, then duck back in – as though it wanted to overtake. So Harjit slowed down to let the car pass. But instead of overtaking him, the car accelerated right up behind Harjit's car until the round headlights filled his rear-view mirror. Then the driver started flashing his headlights.

Harjit changed right down to third gear, then hit the accelerator. The turbo kicked in, sucking air into the engine, and he sped away. Harjit turned the car sharply into a bend, the hedge clipping his wing mirror. But the lights of the car soon appeared behind

him again as it raced to catch up. Harjit saw he was approaching the turn-off to his estate. The other car would surely speed off along the main road. Wouldn't it?

Harjit signalled left and swung his Punto off the main road. The other car closed up right behind him and followed. The car dived out again, then dived in as they approached a blind bend.

The Punto's tyres gripped the slick, wet road at speed. The other driver dropped back to take the corner more slowly. The driver was still flashing the old-fashioned yellow headlights and now blasted on the car's horn.

There was no doubt in Harjit's mind. He was being followed by some crazy driver who was trying to run him off the road. He fumbled in his pocket for his phone. The Punto lurched dangerously across the road, slicing through a deep puddle. Harjit fought to get the car back on the right side of the road.

Harjit hit the speed-dial key for "Home".

"Answer it, someone, come on! Answer it!" he muttered anxiously to himself. Just as he thought it was going to go to answerphone, he heard his dad's voice:

"Harjit? Are you alright?"

"No, Dad, I'm not. I'm coming home. Some crazy puddu's following me!"

"What? OK. Don't stop," Harjit's dad told him. "If he's still behind you when you pull into the drive, your brothers and me will be ready for him."

Harjit cancelled the call and threw the phone onto the passenger seat. The car with the yellow lights had caught right up behind him. The blarring horn turned Harjit's nerves to ice.

The DJ on the radio handed over to the local newsroom. Harjit shuddered when he heard the lead story:

*"Police warn that the convicted killer
who escaped from prison earlier today
is still in the area. A police spokesman
said: 'Members of the public should stay
inside during hours of darkness, and
should lock all sheds and garages. This
man is extremely violent.'"*

With a sudden, sickening feeling of terror, Harjit understood it all. The escaped killer had stolen a car and was now stalking him, trying to make his move; to make him – Harjit – his next victim.

Harjit put his foot down and the turbo wheezed. He had to get away. He had to get home.

Harjit drove as fast as he could. With each bend tyres clawed at the tarmac and gravel spat under the car. The engine wined and the needle on the rev counter shot crazily up and down as Harjit moved rapidly through the gears.

The road ahead was totally deserted. In front of him, the grey rain faded to black in the distance. Every move he made, the car with round yellow lights pursued him; headlights flashing, horn blaring.

The hard ruthless eyes
of the killer...

After what seemed like the longest car journey of his life, Harjit turned sharply into his drive. The lights in the house were all on. Harjit came to a halt and turned off the engine. Incredibly, the other car had followed him up the drive! But great waves of relief washed over him as he sat in his car looking in his rear-view mirror as his dad and brothers raced towards the madman behind him. They pulled open the driver's door.

"What do you think you're doing, terrifying my son like that?" Harjit heard his dad yelling.

"I've been trying to warn him!" the driver

shouted back. He stumbled out of his car, seemingly determined to get to Harjit's Punto. Harjit saw his brothers block him off. Harjit's dad grabbed hold of the man.

"I'm not letting you go. Not until I've handed you over to the police," Harjit's dad growled.

"Don't you understand?" Harjit heard the man plead. "There's an escaped killer on the loose! I saw him crawl into the back of your son's car, over in Welton! I recognised him from the news. We've got to get him before he murders your son!"

Harjit's blood ran cold. He reached out for the door handle, but a split second too late. A large pair of vice-like hands clamped tightly around his neck and jerked his head back. Harjit found himself staring at the rear-view mirror; straight into the hard, ruthless eyes of the killer on the back seat. He tried to scream, but nothing came out. The vice-like hands around his neck were already squeezing the breath from his body.

THE END...

The Babysitter

1

The easiest way to make money ever...

Erin felt a tingle of excitement as she stepped into the large, brightly lit kitchen. This was her very first babysitting job.

"I've put some cans of cola in the fridge for you, Erin. There's pizza too, if you get hungry," said Mrs Baxter. "Now, come upstairs and see the twins. I put them to bed an hour ago. I expect they're asleep by now."

Erin's feet sank into the thick carpet as she followed Mrs Baxter upstairs.

Mrs Baxter gently pushed open the door to the nursery. Inside, Erin saw two matching cots, each with a mobile of the moon and stars dangling above it. Inside each cot there was a sleeping toddler.

"Sophie and Harry," said Mrs Baxter softly.

"They're lovely," whispered Erin. The sight of the twin toddlers, each curled up facing the other, each with a thumb in their mouth, gave her a kind of warm glow inside.

As Erin and Mrs Baxter went back out onto the landing, the door to another room, marked "Office", shot open. A tall man burst out. He was fumbling with his tie.

He glowered at Mrs Baxter. "Are you ready, darling?" he snapped. He ignored Erin completely.

"I was just showing Erin the twins," replied Mrs Baxter.

The man bounded down the stairs. "My husband," explained Mrs Baxter. "He always worries about being late for things."

In the hall, Mr Baxter helped his wife on with her fake fur coat. As he thrust open the front door, a chilly autumn wind blew into the hall.

"We'll be back by 11," Mrs Baxter said.

Mrs Baxter hurried out behind her husband towards the waiting car and quickly closed the door behind her.

Erin went straight to the kitchen, grabbed a can from the fridge and took it into the living room. She sank down into the soft, leather sofa. She found the remote control and switched on the TV. Her best friend Ashley had been right, babysitting was the easiest way to make money ever!

–2–

"Hello? Who's there?"

Erin sat with her feet up on the sofa watching a new US comedy show, while she texted Ashley. She was just about to send it when she heard a chiming sound coming from the table in the corner of the room. The Baxters' phone. Erin tossed her phone down on the sofa, went over and picked up the handset.

"Hello?"

Silence.

"Hello?"

Silence. A faint click, then nothing.

Erin sighed, hung up and went back to the sofa. Probably some insurance company, she

thought. They were always getting calls from them at home. She had just sat down when the Baxters' phone rang again. This time Erin hit the mute button on the TV remote, cutting off the babble of excited young American voices.

She walked over and snatched up the handset.

"Hello?"

Silence.

"Is that you, Ashley?"

Silence. And then the sound of breathing; at first faint, then becoming steady, heavy. Erin couldn't keep the panic from her voice:

"What do you want?" she said loudly.

Silence. Then a man's voice said, "Sing me a lullaby, Erin."

Erin wasn't sure how long she stood there before replying.

"A lullaby?" She could feel her whole body freeze. "Go away, you freak!" She cut the call off. But the phone started ringing again as soon as she put the handset back.

She grabbed the handset and put it to her ear, even though her hand was shaking.

He was singing "Rock-a-bye baby".

Erin cut him off again, and before the chiming could start, she stabbed 999. Her call was answered almost immediately.

"Which service do you require?"

"Police," replied Erin, breathlessly.

Then a woman's voice said, "Can I help you?"

"A man keeps ringing up," blurted out Erin. "Heavy breathing, singing lullabies."

"Hmmm... prank call, huh?"

"No, he knew my name."

"OK. Don't worry, we'll get a trace on the line. It won't take a minute. What's your number?"

Erin read out the number on the telephone base.

"And your name?"

"Erin."

"Are you on your own, Erin?"

Erin thought of Sophie and Harry, sleeping upstairs. "No, there's—"

But before she could explain, the police officer had interrupted her: "That's good. We'll get back to you shortly."

Feeling sick to the pit of her stomach, Erin realised she had to replace the handset if the police were going to be able to call her back.

She slotted the handset on to the base. It didn't ring.

She couldn't sit down. The seconds passed.

Then the phone rang loudly, making her jump. Four rings… Five rings… Six…

Erin's shaking hand hovered over the handset. If she picked it up, what would she hear? The voice of a police officer? Deep breathing? Or the gentle, but menacing tones of a lullaby?

There was fear in the officer's voice...

Erin lifted the handset slowly.

"Hello? Erin? This is the police."

Relief.

"Yes…?"

"We've identified the number from which the nuisance calls are being made."

"Oh, great. Thank you." Erin felt so relieved she wanted to hug someone.

"Who's there with you, Erin?"

"No one. I'm babysitting twin toddlers. They're called Sophie and Harry. There aren't any grown-ups here." The relief she felt was making her gabble, she knew.

"I see. Tell you what, I'll get a woman police officer to call round if you like. What's the address?"

"The house is called 'High Beeches'. It's in Park Avenue—"

Erin heard the police officer catch her breath.

"Erin?" There was fear in the officer's voice. "Did you say the house was called 'High Beeches'?"

"Yes…"

"And it's in Park Avenue?"

"Yes… Why? What's wrong?"

"Erin. The address the nuisance caller's phoning from is the same as yours."

"What? It can't be."

"He's in the house with you!"

Erin froze.

"Are there two phone lines in the house? Erin? Are you there?"

"Yes… Yes, there's an office upstairs." Erin was aware that her voice sounded very, very small.

"Just stay where you are. An armed Rapid Response Team will be with you soon. Until then, I'll stay on the end of the phone. Erin? Erin? Will you answer me, please?"

-4-

Suddenly, she felt her wrist grabbed from behind...

But Erin couldn't answer. Carefully, she had put the handset down on top of the table and had gone across to the other side of the living room.

Now, she just stood and stared at the green light pulsating on the baby alarm. She could just make out the tiny snores of Sophie and Harry asleep upstairs. Any minute she expected to hear the snores turn to screams. But maybe, she thought, he would murder them silently in their sleep. She stood there playing things through her mind. Mr and Mrs Baxter had paid her to look after their children. They were her responsibility. It was her job to take care of them!

Her legs trembling, Erin tiptoed through to the kitchen. If she was going to tackle the intruder, she would need to be armed, she knew. She slipped one of the kitchen knives out of the rack on the wall. Only then did she notice that another of the knives was missing – she'd have sworn it was there earlier. She stood there staring at the empty slot. Terrified but determined, she eventually turned and made her way into the hall.

As Erin climbed the stairs, each footstep she took sank noiselessly into the carpet. She stopped on each stair and listened: nothing but the thud of her heart and a pounding in her ears.

At the top Erin saw the door to the nursery, slightly open. Beyond it, just along the landing, was the door marked "Office", where she knew the intruder must be, lying in wait with a kitchen knife.

She tiptoed towards the nursery door, all the while keeping one eye on the office door. Her fingers were sticky with sweat as they gripped the handle of the knife.

Quietly, she reached the nursery and put out her free hand to push the door open. Suddenly, she felt her wrist grabbed from behind and another hand clamped over her mouth.

Before she could scream, she was hauled backwards across the landing and into Mr and Mrs Baxter's bedroom. She struggled wildly, but the powerful grip on her wrist tightened and the knife slipped to the floor. A black-booted foot kicked it out of the way under the bed.

She was swung round and found herself staring into the taut face of the man who was holding her: a face that was framed by a black balaclava.

As she tried desperately to pull away, she saw the word POLICE printed across the front of the man's flak jacket.

"Don't move!" the police officer growled, just as someone out on the landing shouted, "Armed Police! You, inside the office. Come out with your hands up!"

Then came the sound of hammering and splintering of wood, and another cry: "Armed Police! Drop the knife! Do it now!"

A loud, hollow gunshot made Erin squeal, and it was quickly followed by a deep howl of pain from somewhere outside the room.

There was a moment's silence, then the increasingly anxious cries of two terrified young children began to fill the air.

THE END...

DEADLY TALES

One book.
Two nightmares.

978 1 4451 0340 2 pb
978 1 4451 0855 1 eBook

978 1 4451 0337 2 pb
978 1 4451 0852 0 eBook

978 1 4451 0341 9 pb
978 1 4451 0856 8 eBook

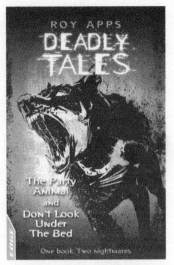

978 1 4451 0339 6 pb
978 1 4451 0854 4 eBook

978 1 4451 0338 9 pb
978 1 4451 0851 3 eBook

Find out more about these books and
others published by EDGE at:
www.franklinwatts.co.uk

Plus visit Roy's website for the latest
news on all his books:
www.royapps.co.uk

DEADLY TALES
TEASER

Can't wait to find out what happens in the other DEADLY TALES urban legends? Well, here's a teaser from

The Bloody Hook:

Voices – jeering, yelling; getting closer. Keisha pulled away from Leon, wiped her hand on the misted-up window. The car park was empty, except for a gang of six figures. They were waving bottles in the air, weaving their way towards Leon's car.

The Warlords.

One of them walked ahead of the others. He was larger than the rest. Leon looked round in time to see the street light catch on something shiny where his right hand should be. But it wasn't a bottle. It was a meat hook.

The Butcher.

Keisha screamed as the back window was hit with something heavy. By the time Leon had fired up the engine, the Warlords had surrounded the car, pushing their noses tight against the windows, growling and snarling like crazed animals. They smashed their bottles against the windscreen, and kicked the doors. As Leon let out the clutch and screeched away, two figures leapt onto the bonnet, grabbing at the windscreen wipers. Leon frantically spun the car round and they rolled off onto the ground.

The Butcher swung his hook at Keisha's window and the glass exploded. Keisha cried out and grabbed the door's armrest with both hands. She had to stop him getting in!

✝

Dare you to read the rest in:
DEADLY TALES
The Bloody Hook
and
Vanishing Hitchhiker

Want to read more horror? Try iHorror by The 2Steves, where you are the hero and have to choose your own fate.

Fight your fear. Choose your fate.

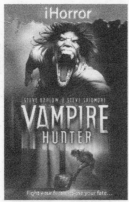

978 1 40830 985 8 pb
978 1 40831 476 0 eBook

978 1 40830 986 5 pb
978 1 40831 477 7 eBook

978 1 40830 988 9 pb
978 1 40831 479 1 eBook

978 1 40830 987 2 pb
978 1 40831 478 4 eBook

Hooked on the DS McAvoy series?
Look out for

TAKING PITY

DS MCAVOY: BOOK 4

David Mark

DS Aector McAvoy's family is in hiding. He has lost his way.

His boss Trish Pharaoh gives him a distraction in the form of an old case. The Winn family was killed forty years ago: were the police right about who pulled the trigger?

But McAvoy's enemies – the ruthless criminal organisation known as the Headhunters – are pitiless. They plan to take everything from those that stand in their way.

And his cold case is strangely linked with the fire that's about to rain down on Hull . . .

Now the ruthless criminal network that has tightened its stranglehold on Hull intends to take everything that remains from those who dare to stand in its way.

OUT NOW IN PAPERBACK AND EBOOK

MULHOLLAND
BOOKS
HODDER

"And just how did you catch prostate cancer?"

Wednesday 14th October 2015

The train is delayed in Penryn and I am sitting at a table seat staring at my notebook. Normally I would be writing down thoughts and ideas, remembering good times and smiling, but today, for some reason, I am feeling utterly useless. I was up early. I had to get to the surgery by 8.30am for my three monthly 'Prostap' injection. I can usually forget about my cancer but this date with a needle is a gentle reminder. That's not the reason for my despair though. Yesterday Bet was in a very distressed state and I fear that she may be again today. I had found her in bed, angry, and adamant that she had had no food. She hated the place and wanted to go home. She claimed that she had been left on top of a chimneystack and wanted to get out of bed. The staff obliged, as they always did, but she was rude to them and verbally abusive. I feared these echoes of the past. I hoped that today I would find her calm and more content.

I write now. I am trying to analyse how I feel at this point of my journey. Why do I now feel so inadequate? I suppose I have been 'in control' for so long now and having to make rapid decisions to the ever-changing scenario that I now realise that I have delegated Bet's care totally to other people. Long-term planning is now out of any equation and my decisions are reduced to 'What do I cook for supper?' or 'What fruit shall I surprise Bet with today?' Even the train journey, initially special and different, has become tedious – and today it is annoying, as we seem stranded in Penryn.

We eventually move and reach that now so familiar platform 1. I reluctantly climb up the hill and I tentatively peer round into Bet's room. The relief I feel when I sense that she is calm is so welcome. She is looking forward to the crushed strawberries although today I notice that she is finding swallowing these increasingly difficult. They collect at the back of her throat and eventually she wretches and the coagulated remains are spit out. Am I right to have decided that we will not go down the route of tube feeding? This problem will increase and inevitably cause further distress. Here am I, feeling sorry for myself for no longer having any 'control' and yet I have made the decision to potentially shorten Bet's life. For two years I have struggled to make sense of our life together and now I feel tired and so uncertain. I am afraid. Am I capable of deciding anything? I know, like all those other thousands of people who care for their loved ones with all forms of dementia, that one can never anticipate. There can be no right or wrong. No matter how prepared one is – there will be sudden and totally outrageous reaction, which strikes a blow to the heart.

One of my heart cutting moments occurred shortly after Bet had returned home from 'Crossroads'. For a couple of days all had appeared calm but on this particular morning Bet had become increasing agitated about the fact that we would soon have to move from our home. We were walking along the main street, the sun was shining, and there were crowds of people around. It was one of those mornings when we would, months previously, have told ourselves again how lucky we were to live in Falmouth with its lively students and its fresh sea air. Today though, Bet was angry; her limp was pronounced, and she walked some distance away from me. As we walked past The Poly, where a few months before I had 'organised' the box office and trained new volunteers, she turned and screamed at me.

"And how did you catch prostate cancer? You caught it from sleeping around! You didn't catch it from me!" With that she turned back to focus on her journey, increased her speed – and left me stunned.

There now seemed to be a very determined effort, on Bet's part, to reassert some form of autonomy. She was adamant that she no longer needed to take the prescription drugs. She no longer feared 'the knives' so, in her mind, there was no longer any need for the 'tickle of psychiatric hocus pocus'. I had to find devious ways to counter her devious ways! I would find her tablets hidden under the carpet or pushed into the rubbish bin and I would try, in vain, to negotiate with her or try to reason. A waste of my time! Our GP however, displayed a remarkable cou d'e-tat , a wonderful slight of mind, when she promised to prescribe drugs to alleviate Bet's ever-increasing fear of constipation – on condition that Bet continued to take the other set of tablets. Bet agreed! How impressed was I! And how relieved! For a few months, at least, Bet would take her pills – although never willingly nor without question:

I wish he would stop these pills for me – it seems as though they are essential... Pete seems to think I am miserable. I've taken the bloody tablets. It should be a great time but not when Pete says rude things about me... Bet Kaye 28th April 2015

And apparently not without me appearing to be in 'control'! Of some things anyway. My treatment, with its 'chemical castration' as one young doctor accurately and honestly described it, was obviously slowing me down in one department:

Tea at 7.15am and then a very strange 'love' with self-orgasm. What have we come to? We went into town to collect my prescription which the doctor still insists that I take! What have I come to! I feel exactly the same as I have always felt but now we are both on stupid medication. I feel bludgeoned into something I don't need! Drugs! Pete may be ill but he's not the man I married. He doesn't fulfil my needs really apart from keeping a check on where I go! I must stop writing like this and moaning. I feel so helpless in this situation...
Bet Kaye 6 May 2015

Friends rallied round to help me try to maintain some sanity. Ann and Kevin invited us for suppers and Bet enjoyed her after dinner whisky by their log burner. We arranged another 'jolly' and booked our rail tickets to Dawlish where we would meet up with Anne and Derek – old friends from our Scarborough days. Derek lectures in archaeology at Exeter University and had been closely involved in the boat building project at Falmouth Maritime Museum in which Kevin had been a willing volunteer 'chippy'. Anne had been a teacher of Latin and Classics in Scarborough Girl's High school but she adapted so easily and enthusiastically when the school became the mixed comprehensive with its peg board timetable. I was very keen to create a more integrated approach in the early secondary years and avoid the usual individual subject slots which to me seemed artificial and often restrictive boxes. Anne was such a positive member of our team as classical studies became fun for all and every child got a taste of Latin and its relevance to our language and our modern lives. Why should we make decisions about a child's education at the age of eleven? I suppose that is why I was such a fan of the National Curriculum when the concept was first mooted. All children had the right to be introduced to all aspects of life – and only then could they make decisions about their future. That was my mantra for thirty years and I followed my star with great joy until it shattered into an explosion of League Tables and SATS!

Bet was on good form and appeared to be enjoying her day. Her diary makes reference to 'The Ten Green Bottles' where she enjoyed 'fish cake, salad and chips'.

After lunch our hosts took us a walk around the town. Bet tried so hard to remain independent and I could see how she was struggling to conceal her 'clumpy leg' and avoid relying on too much support from me. The approach up to Anne and Derek's cottage is up a steep flight of steps. Half way up Bet fell backwards. Luckily Kevin was behind her and his cricketing reflexes took over and he caught her. She does refer to this in her diary but adds 'it has been a lovely day with our lovely friends'. I am so glad that we continued to make an effort to involve Bet in life as it had been.

Whenever I meet Dawlish Anne I remember that our children had always called her the 'pin lady'! In one of my productions – "Dracula Spectacular" – Anne had created a huge safety pin which appeared to hold her head onto her body. Funny, isn't it, how some images remain so clear! The 'School Play' had always been such an important part of my school life. And thankfully I've had the good fortune to work in schools which appreciated the value of drama in all its forms. Even 'Chung Hua' in Sibu, Sarawak didn't escape my thespian tenacity way back in 1965. There I had decided to introduce my Chinese students to "The Man Who Married the Dumb Wife" by Anatoile France – partly because I remembered it well as I had played the lead back at Hemsworth – but I felt that the story would be understood by the visual content – even if our audience wouldn't understand our attempts at the English Language. It was fun and I held my cast in admiration for their bravery. On my return home Bet would from now onwards always be by my side, quietly guiding my direction and making costume and props with great skill. I doubt if she ever realised how much I came to rely on her – for, sadly, I doubt if I ever told her.

Bet had been in productions at Spilsby Grammar – although she never found the smell of the greasepaint as addictive as I did. I was in every play possible whilst at school. Not content with the traditional annual school plays and the House Drama Festivals I persuaded a group of friends to form a Sixth Form Drama Club. One of our gang, Fran, had suffered from polio as a youngster which had confined her to wearing callipers. Bless her! She volunteered her services to transport our set and costumes in, on and around her three wheel mobility scooter whilst the rest of us struggled to keep up by the local buses. We offered our production, a farce of course, to any local group or charity – in return for the use of a performance area and that led us in interesting directions. The 'highlight' has to be Rossington Miners' Gala where, on a very hot afternoon, we were led into a large marquee with a gigantic stage. Then the audience was released and in poured hundreds of children for their afternoon's entertainment. We were the 'child minders' – and had any of my friends gone on to become stand up comedians then this would have been engraved in their memory as a gig to be remembered. I did try to become a serious actor. I auditioned for Prospero in The South Yorkshire Theatre for Youth but was asked to play Trinculo – the gangly body and the lark-legs struck again! No one talked to me about any possibility of a career in the theatre and I had no idea how one should go about such a thing. At that stage I was applying to university to study Geography. Three good passes at A level were required and my plans were shattered when the Mathematics teachers refused to enter me for A level. I had always been considered to be very good at 'Maths' but I missed the introductory lessons to 'calculus' at the beginning of the Sixth Form – and from that point on I struggled to understand much of the course. My teachers were brilliant mathematicians but they failed to be able to understand my quandary. I wasn't that brilliant either in my A level English classes and the general consensus was that 'drama' and 'playing the fool' were my academic downfall. The realisation that I couldn't now get onto a Geography degree course hit me hard. Career Guidance at Hemsworth Grammar School consisted of a shelf of books in the school library and they gave me little succour. For a brief moment the idea of becoming a 'purser', with a carefree life on the ocean, attracted my travel buds. Then one of my Maths teachers, feeling sympathy for the almost blubbering lost sole in front of him, crouched down beside me and talked to me about a career in 'teaching'. He told me about the new teacher training courses, now three years in length, which were being introduced at degree level. That was my road to Damascus moment.

And so, with just my two A levels, I began my three years at Coventry College of Education.

Why Coventry? It had a swimming pool and I really

did need to learn to swim. And it had a good reputation in Drama. I didn't quite have the courage to study Drama as a main subject – and I kept Geography to the fore. Bet began a year as a trainee teacher in Lincolnshire and then she too came to Coventry. Again I threw myself into performing whenever the opportunity arose – 'Rio Rita' in 'The Hostage' and 'Geoffrey' in 'A Taste of Honey' – always the sensitive part – never the tough lead! A group of us decided to take a production up to the Edinburgh Festival – the first time a College of Education had performed on The Fringe. Bet was part of that pioneering team and willingly became our sound engineer. The night that the tape recorder reel to reel spewed out tape in all directions is still a vivid memory. A lesser a mortal would have panicked – but not Bet. In the dark she patiently rewound the pile of spaghetti and not a cue was missed.

I aim for inclusion in school plays – just as in all aspects of school life. In practice this can lead to a rather over-crowded stage. At Cudworth Secondary there are colourful images which bring a smile. My 'Peter Pumpernickle' in 'Trudi and the Minstrel' by Alan Cullen, actually wet himself during the performance – and from the wings, down the rake of the stage, we watched as the trickle reached the edge and crept towards the audience. That poor little stage almost collapsed under the weight of the hordes of budding actors who trod the boards in Brecht's 'Caucasian Chalk Circle'. I'm not sure my cast fully appreciated the 'alienation techniques' but they enjoyed themselves and that was my aim. I'm sure a touch of socialism would have rubbed off for I was quite proud of my growing reputation as a left wing trendy who placed creativity way above punctuation. I think I agree with Brecht's philosophy "Art is not a mirror with which to reflect reality but a hammer with which to shape it." At the end of my teaching career Brecht was again to feature significantly in my life. I enjoyed teaching A Level 'Theatre Studies' so much.

I am sure Bet would have made most of the costumes for my productions at Cudworth. She also threw herself wholeheartedly into making mini-pinies for Naples. The travel bug, ever competing within me, had led me to taking a group of students to live and work for a few weeks at an orphanage in Naples. Way before 'risk assessment' had stilted imaginative adventures I had decided that there were far better ways for young people to appreciate life in a foreign land other than via the conventional school trip in the organised coach and with the over-cautious itinerary. I had initially made contact with a Father Borelli, a Catholic priest who ran a home for homeless boys in Napoli and we began to raise money with enthusiasm. Sadly Father Borelli wrote to say that he would greatly appreciate the money but certainly didn't want any help from a motley crew from a Secondary Modern School in South Yorkshire. Just when I thought that I had perhaps been a little over-ambitious I was pointed in the direction of Casa Materna. This was a Methodist organisation run by the Santi Family. What a difference! What a welcome! What an experience for us all!

We spent months in preparation raising money and begging for paint, clothing and food. Bet had thrown herself whole-heartedly into all aspects of the project. It seemed as though she was a member of staff at Cudworth – and yet I know that she was carving out her own career at a school miles away. And I know that post at Upton was very demanding – and I know that she took her responsibilities seriously and did the very best that she could to improve the life chances of youngsters from quite a deprived area. It is now, that I look back, that I can fully appreciate just how hard she worked. I certainly couldn't have achieved my aims without her. Together we took our group of fourteen and fifteen year olds to Luton airport where a travel company had given us a very generous 'deal' and were flying us to Rome. History teacher Jennie, part of the advance party had set off in Geography teacher Ken's landrover loaded with paint, soups, clothing and many other gifts which had been so willingly donated by local families and companies.

We spent a few days camping near to Sorento with a few of the older boys from Casa Materna. Friendships struck up immediately and the atmosphere was so supportive and positive. We knew it was going to be a success. We then moved into the orphanage itself and set about painting the classrooms – and playing football! We joined in with the music and the art activities – and the staff drove us in their bus to Vesuvius, Pompeii and Herculaneum. We sensed that the most delicate area of our stay would be around food and I anticipated that not all my urchins would bond with orphanage cuisine. This was before the days of takeaways and supermarket shelves labelled 'Foreign Foods' and we suspected, quite rightly, that these first time travellers from the mining villages of South Yorkshire would not quite take to bowls of pasta. And so I had arranged for us to camp in Rome for a few days before flying home and I had discovered a camp site which boasted a 'fish and chip shop'. I make no apology for using bribery. "Eat the pasta, my angels, and you can have fish and chips every day in Rome!" As we drove into the camp site we hit a traffic jam. A fire engine dashed in front of us and there was a terrific explosion. You've guessed it! That was the end of the chip shop and the end of my promise. Despite this set back the adventure proved to be so rewarding for us all. Above all my students became close friends with Italian children and they lived along side them and for a few weeks were able to share their lives. We had painted a few classrooms and had bought them shoes and clothes – and in return they had offered us a home, food, laughter and friendship. And Bet was there in the middle of it all, ever smiling and oozing confidence. I felt that we had achieved this together. I hope she realised that too.

Mrs Oxley did all she could to make my work at Cudworth fulfilling. For a year the Head of English was seconded and I was offered the role which I grabbed with enthusiasm. I had now decided that it was English and Drama that I wanted to teach and ox bow lakes and karst scenery were a distant blur. I studied for an English Literature degree with the Open University which was not easy as I tried to slot in assignments with drama productions and money raising for Italy. I would find myself having to spend every minute of the annual residential courses catching up with essays. Always I was the conscience of the group! The bar rarely touched my lips. But the result was, I suppose, that by the time I became Head of English at Darfield Foulstone High I had, almost, a degree in the subject! Only when I retired from teaching twenty five years later did I discover that my hard-earned degree had never made it onto my 'official record'! Hmm!

Harry Herdman had recently taken over the Headship of Foulstone as it changed from secondary modern to comprehensive. What an exciting time that was – where the equal value principle reigned supreme and financial investment in schools was seen as a key to the country's future. I went to meet Harry before I applied. I set before him my vision. Every child was an individual and needed to believe that they were each of worth. I would encourage values of compassion, tolerance and understanding. Drama would be at the centre of my department's approach as, through self expression, we would aim to build up self confidence. I would place creativity above all else. When any child feels valued and is encouraged to contribute his or her ideas – then there would be a desire to express those ideas correctly. Grammar had its place – but it certainly wasn't going to be where my department would start. It was a risk, I realised, as Harry twiddled with his glasses and tapped them on his desk. But I was thrilled with his response. He hoped that I would apply and that he would do all in his power to give me the staff who would respond with enthusiasm. I applied and found myself working with a young team who had almost all trained in English and Drama at Bretton Hall. The next four years will remain the highlight of my teaching career. We taught as a team – often working with the whole year group of 120/ 150 pupils, offering choices wherever possible. We linked with any other area of the curriculum where the teachers were brave enough to leave behind the restrictions of four walls and a blackboard. I thought it was wonderful – but remember I was 'a left wing trendy'! No doubt some looked on with horror! There is no right and wrong way to 'educate' just as there is no clear pathway to successful parenting. At the centre though, must be the individual child. I think that is why I have avoided 'setting' or, even more damaging in my opinion, 'streaming' – although I accept the need for such devices in certain areas of knowledge. Bet and I would often share our views on individuality – and the balance that was necessary for both of us. Bet would be moulding her four year olds – all unique from a variety of backgrounds – into a coherent community. I would be wanting freedom of expression – and yet having to accept that freedom is comparative – and my drama classes needed strict discipline.

My time at Darfield was warm and comfortable for

other reasons. Our daughters joined our family, Yong came over from Malaysia to study A levels and our lovely new bungalow responded well to our increase in numbers – and Bet kept us all happy. She made the decision not to return to teaching whilst the children were young but she continued to be an integral part of my work. She made it a priority to know my team and their families and we became a group of good friends. As I look back I recognise how much influence Bet had on my career. She was my advisor and my critic – in many ways she was my inspiration. She had always as much time as I required. I realise now how patient she must have been as I continued to tread the boards at the same time as she struggled with two very young children. Darfield also provided me with some thespian highlights. I directed "Oh What a Lovely War" and played Willy Mossop in "Hobson's Choice". It also provided me my only 'starring role' in a musical. I was directing "Oliver" as a joint staff-pupil production. Nils was brilliantly playing the part of Fagin but, sadly, during rehearsals, his father died. The funeral was scheduled for our opening night and I had to make a decision. Either I cancelled the opening or I stepped into the role myself! I am no singer but Fagin can get away with almost speaking his songs. I would have a go! Lyrics are the key of course. As an actor one can improvise – but not so with a song. One fluff and the whole song falls apart. So I spent the day learning the songs, and placing cue sheets in various places – inside the frying pan, on the linings of Fagin's ragged coat, on the back of the brazier – wherever

Fagin was on stage there would be the relevant lyrics. What I failed to realise was that under the intense glare of stage lighting I would not be able to focus on them. I was on my own! For a moment I felt that this was to be the end of my theatrical career! My teaching career perhaps! But the orchestra struck up and so did I. I got through without a stumble. An absolute bag of nerves – but the audience knew nothing of my dilemma and the reviews were good. I so wanted to play the part again and this time I would be able to enjoy it! But Nils came back and it was important to him to be able to get back into his routine. He still remembers finding my cue sheets under the sausages.

I found myself directing 'Oliver' once again in Scarborough after we moved our family to live beside the sea. The Graham School enabled me to meet up with Bill Scott – a great musician who also understood the stage. The Graham also boasted a wonderful stage and school hall with multi levels and even a balcony. Our imaginative stage designer, John Dunwell, made the most of the unique shape and constructed a bridge over the London rooftops! As a production team we were rather anxious as opening night approached, Hilda Briggs, our Head Teacher, had been, until the creation of comprehensive schools two years previously, head of the Girls'High School and that school had a reputation for very high dramatic standards. Her ex High School staff would constantly warn us that Hilda would not warm to our style. We proved them wrong of course, and at the final performance, where the audience were invited to come along in Victorian costume, Hilda entered totally into the spirit and came as a remarkably accurate Queen Victoria! She 'knighted' me at the final curtain. Drama was safely to the fore in her 'new' school.

We had to find another musical for the following year – and that is how we came to find 'Dracula Spectacula' and how Anne, now living in Dawlish, came to be known as the 'pin lady'! We have photographs of Becca and Sam in black cloaks and scary masks – for from a very early age my family became an integral part of the Scott Kaye musical age. Bet's name is always listed on our programmes –usually under costume or design. What the programme never credits though, is that she held me up. She made me believe in myself. When we came to despair that there was so little of value being published for school production, she was the first to encourage us to write our own. And that is what we did!

I began to write a script based on the story of Gladys Aylward – the missionary who had led a group of Chinese children over the mountains to safety. I had loved the film "The Inn of the Sixth Happiness' and thought that it was an ideal theme for a school musical. I also read "The Small Woman" by Alan Burgess. The thrill of writing lyrics, passing them to Bill, and then listening to a beautiful song was a new experience for me – and I was to be hooked. Bill and I were to create a further six full length musicals over the next six years. Our first show, which we titled 'The Inn of Happiness' found its way into the hands of Evans Brothers who at that time were publishing school musical shows. They thought that is was a brilliant and effective show and would have loved to publish it. However, they also had published 'The Small Woman' and Alan Burgess had claimed the 'right's to Gladys Aylward's story and was not prepared to allow us to publish. There was an 'off the record' suggestion that we should go ahead and publish it ourselves. There was a feeling that Alan Burgess would not challenge us if it were to become a potential court case. Such an idea, of course, was totally beyond us. This was way before word processors – never mind the internet and self publication. We were also full time teachers. Any spare time we had was now focussing on next year's production. We had been 'hoisted by our own petard' and expectations were high. Bill and I had to come up with something bigger and hopefully better.

'Our Finest Hour' was certainly bigger. This story of evacuees from London during the Second World War created parts for as many youngsters who wanted to take part. We wrote our shows to give maximum 'work' to our chorus – and back stage must have been a nightmare of organisation and stage discipline. Thankfully that was rarely my scene! One of the perks of the director is that he can watch from the back row! My thanks will always be to the hundreds of colleagues who have suffered to make the shows run so smoothly! Evans Brothers loved our music – but they felt that our story was too serious! They had successfully published 'Dracula Spectacular' and asked us to write something in a similar style. Bill and I were reluctant. We both felt that a school musical was such an excellent way of getting over worthy themes. Our next show 'The Coyote and The Locust' dealt with the Battle of the Wounded Knee and the way in which the North America Indians had suffered at the hands of the white men. Our friends at Evans Brothers now pleaded with us. Could we take a familiar character or story, 'send it up' and make sure there were several laughs on every page! That's how 'Rock on Henry' came to be written. Even then we couldn't reduce Henry VIII to a figure of ridicule and there was much poignancy in the finished show. Bet did all the research for me and invested so much time and energy into helping to make it such a successful production. Evans Brothers were delighted with us and gave us a time and date to make a phone call to their London Office. It seemed a strange route to have to follow but I remember that call so clearly. They had just been taken over by Samuel French. It would be little consolation, they knew, but they wanted us to know that they would have published "Rock on Henry". All they could do was to pass on our work to the new regime with the recommendation that publication should be made. We then began a relationship with a new London Team and were in discussion over points of costume and setting detail. It was all so positive. With hind sight I played the wrong card for I sent them a copy, fresh off the 'Gestetner' (stencil dupicator!), of our latest show. The new one was called 'Oh Nell' and was based on the life of Nell Gwynn. This caused a delay, for the publishing team now spent weeks deliberating about which to publish first. Then the cruellest blow of all. The company withdrew its budget for school musicals. We had never set out to publish but we were now bitterly disappointed. We had a collection of appealing and challenging shows and we wanted more young people to enjoy taking part in them. Today there is access to them on line – but back in the 70's we had no way of reaching a mass audience. Scarborough Operatic Society did perform both 'Rock on Henry!' and 'The Inn of Happiness' which gave me the opportunity to direct at The Stephen Joseph Theatre and for a brief moment in time I could feel that I was in competition with Alan Ayckbourn. What might have been!

When we moved down to Cornwall I continued to work with drama – and I like to think that it was with the same degree of enthusiastic fervour. Sam and Becca were always involved which was comforting for me – but Bet was no longer such an integral part. As I look back now I realise that she was no longer part of my school family – but the close team work I had known in Yorkshire was now missing. Perhaps as Deputy Head I was inevitably tarnished as 'senior management' with its inherent barriers? More likely it came down to geography and the fact that our students and staff led lives which were widely scattered over many miles of Bodmin Moor and surrounding hamlets. I do remember the Head of PE telling me, shortly after I arrived, that I had no chance of establishing large scale productions as all the lads would be too busy playing rugby! I proved him wrong!

In Cornwall Bet was now to focus on looking after our extended family at 'Rylands'.

For the past year I have witnessed Bet, as though struggling to place a value on her life, telling every one – doctors, carers, social workers, psychiatrists, post men and Uncle Tom Cobley and all :

"I looked after our parents and our children – the most important thing!"

No one would ever dispute that my love. But don't forget that you held me up too! And by the way, I never did 'sleep around'!

"I want a wee!"

Saturday 24th October 2015

Today is rather special. Sam, Joe and Katie are with me. We are heading up the corridor towards Bet's room carrying our picnic lunch. This afternoon we have tickets to see the touring production of 'Lord of the Flies' adapted from William Golding's novel. This is directed by Tim Shearder – director of Regent's Park Open Air Theatre. Tim was at primary school with Sam and Becca and I think I can claim to have directed him in his first musical when he was one of the small children rescued by Gladys Aylward when Scarborough Operatic Society performed "The Inn of Happiness". This will be our second visit to The Hall for Cornwall this week. On Wednesday we went to see 'Jesus Christ Super Star' and both Joe and Katie enjoyed that. I would like to keep their interest flourishing in the musical theatre world. A couple of years ago Bet had started to teach them both the piano but somehow neither of them really wanted to continue and Bet was not her usual patient self. With hindsight we now know that all was not well.

Bet is in her chair and seems pleased to see the children. They collect their sandwiches and Joe goes off to one of the quiet, newly refurbished lounges where he can watch the television in peace. Katie quietly and fairly discretely begins to 'do gymnastics' on Bet's bed but Sam and I focus on Bet's routine and all goes without too much anxiety. We both notice how Bet's ability to drink is now deteriorating rapidly. She tends to slurp and choke. There is always water in the room but it is difficult to know how often the care staff can pop in and moisten her lips. She never complains though. I think back to the previous year when she was adamant that everyone should drink at least three litres of water a day.

Another belief had turned into an obsession. When Bet returned home from 'Crossroads' in the spring of 2014 she would go nowhere without a water bottle clutched in her hand or in her bag. She would stop frequently, struggle sometimes to open the bottle, and take a huge swig. She had rightly always seen a healthy need to keep up the water intake but it was now becoming an addiction. If we set off towards town without her water then I would have to go home and collect it – or buy her a new bottle from the nearest shop. At the same time she would remonstrate with me that I wasn't drinking enough. Here was I waiting for a date for a TURP procedure (as operations now seem to be called) so that my bladder might empty properly. This was to become the summer of the bladders. Obviously, as Bet drank more and more, her need for the loo increased in direct proportion. As I didn't always have the best of control either our journeys became more and more dependant on the availability of public toilets.

It was June 2014 when we moved out of Arwenack Avenue. In those few weeks before our move Bet came more and more closer to accepting that we had no choice. Her diaries recognise that all is not well – although there is never any real understanding of how difficult it was for me:

> *This afternoon we've been down to Events Square to hear the sea shanties. I needed to sit down for a bit and Pete bought me a drink but then couldn't find me as I felt tired and wanted to come home ...*
> Bet Kaye 14 June 2014

The reality had been slightly more dramatic as far as I had experienced. We had arrived in the crowded square and sat, in the sun, on some steps giving us a good view of the stage and the singers. As soon as we sat down Bet demanded a drink. I went over to the bar, about thirty yards away, and for a few minutes Bet was out of my sight. I returned with our drinks – but she had gone. There was just no sign of her. Other people were now sitting in the space she had vacated – but they couldn't remember seeing where Bet had gone. There were thousands of folk now in the square. I quickly downed my pint, and still clutching Bet's apple juice, I began to trawl my eyes through the crowds. I met up with Wendy and Gordon and they too began to search. She had done this to me before of course, but I still had no idea where, or how, she would eventually turn up. After about ten minutes of frantic crowd scanning Kevin found us. He and Ann had been on their way to the square and had discovered Bet standing outside the public toilets.

Apparently she had been for 'a wee' and then had no idea where I was or what we were doing. Ann had stayed with her and Kevin had come to find us. The loos are a few hundred yards away but obviously Bet knew exactly where to find them. She didn't want to return to the singing and so I walked her gently home. This was how it was to be for the next few months. I had to keep a close eye on Bet. I felt that I couldn't really leave her alone.

As we, or rather I, packed up boxes for our move, we needed to take some rubbish out to the recycling centre. Bet got out to help and struggled to lift one of the sacks. She insisted on helping, however, and dragged it to the relevant skip. I carried on emptying the car. I then realised that Bet wasn't sitting in the car as I had expected. She was nowhere to be seen. Had she fallen into one of the skips? Her walking was now very unsteady so I assumed she had fallen somewhere. A couple of the staff joined me in searching along the line of skips. No sign of her – and yet she had disappeared in less than a minute. Then I found her. She was sitting in the front passenger seat of another car. It was completely different in colour and style and she had moved the owner's belongings in order to sit down. She climbed out quite amicably when I collected her and I apologised profusely to the lady owner who had now returned. Her diary simply reflects the incident:

I felt a bit silly at the tip as I got into someone else's car, but we've got rid of a lot of stuff...
Bet Kaye 20th June 2014

A couple of days before our move Bet fell backwards down the steps again. This time there was no cricketer to catch her and her body was contorted in a heap to such an extent that I feared for her life. Although dazed she appeared to have control of her limbs and I was able to help her to her feet. It seemed that nothing was broken. Bruising however was severe. It is at times like this that carers must feel vulnerable. Here I was, my wife often claiming that I wanted to kill her, with her body black and blue! Thankfully my relationship with Social Services had so far been positive. Bet had returned from Scorrier, where of course she had been encouraged to see herself as a member of the caring staff, wanting to continue to do care work. R, our social worker, had arranged for Bet to return to 'Crossroads' for one day each week. I would take Bet over in the morning, and son in law Ian would collect her in the evening on his way home from work. This would give me respite time – or that was the theory! Bet decided that just a couple of hours was all she needed and wanted me to take her over after lunch and then collect her two hours later. As the drive over to Scorrier took at last half an hour each way – this would hardly provide me with any 'respite'! Bet could not understand that I needed time alone and it wasn't easy for me to negotiate a suitable compromise. She wasn't too happy but agreed to go over before lunch and that Ian would bring her home again. Each Wednesday I managed a few hours to catch up with shopping at least! And Bet enjoyed her drives home with her son in law. They sang together!

There were other suggestions as to how Bet might like to get involved with groups. Not all were successful.

Today we've been to the Day Centre – but they were all very elderly and slept a lot – but at least we – well I – sang!
Bet Kaye 20th September 2014

Bet did enjoy singing and we had two very interesting musical 'activities'. A 'memory café' met every Tuesday afternoon in a church, which was quite near to our new flat. Every other week this was a 'singing session' with a keyboard player. My intention had been to drop Bet off and collect her again two hours later. Hmm! The toilet was quite a walk down the corridor and Bet wanted me to stay with her for the first session so that I could help her when she 'needed a wee'! So that then became part of my routine too – and I joined in the singing and eventually introduced Beatle songs into the repertoire! Great fun! Then Bet decided that she would like to sing in the Community Choir, which met every week in the Methodist Church in town. Again I hoped that I could sign Bet in and then collect her two hours later. No 'respite' here either. On our initial visit I discovered that the choir consisted of about sixty women but only had four men! The ladies surrounded me and there was no escape. The choir met on the top floor and thankfully there was a lift. The disabled toilet was down on the ground floor and I spent most of the two hour session, which had cost me four pounds each, taking Bet up and down between the floors – for after almost every song she had decided that she 'wanted a wee'! She was now drinking water at an alarming rate but it was impossible to stop her. To even suggest quietly that she should perhaps limit her intake would result in a very angry outburst, which would be distressing to witness. I needed to keep things as calm as I could.

I know the medical team who supported us were concerned about me – and I am indeed very grateful for their care. I was now scheduled to have the TURPS procedure later in the summer. For those of you who are fortunate enough never to have even heard of this operation let me explain. It is designed to burn away part of the prostate which is constricting the urine flow from the bladder and my consultant, very sensibly' wanted me to have a 'good stream' before I began radiotherapy. I'll return to this later! Promise! But at this point in early summer we had moved into a rented flat with level access and it was in my interest to try to get some rest, to find time to relax and to avoid stress and anxiety. Hmm!

Music sessions didn't give me the quiet time that I had hoped for so I began to search other possible avenues. Perhaps I could bring in someone to help me keep the flat in its pristine state? Trish came along. She had experience of dealing with relatives who had dementia and was not phased by Bet's intolerance. Bet was furious with me. We did not need a cleaner! I was quite capable of looking after every thing! Trish managed a few sessions and I was able to escape to

M&S or Sainsbury's for my weekly dose of 'respite' and 'relaxation'! Bet would be rude or become silent. There was no way she would engage with Trish and so that idea was hit on the head. Bet was now writing stories – about an eight-year-old boy called Jed. She would scribble these out and then ask me to type them. Now she wanted them illustrating and, as Jed had befriended a family of dragons, she had a clear idea in her mind of the kind of creatures she wanted to be drawn. Sam had quite a few friends who were artists and I hoped that they could spend a few hours each week working with Bet on bringing her stories to visual life. We tried two – both with art degrees and both recognised as having successfully illustrated children's books. Another great idea! Bet dismissed both within minutes of meeting them. Their illustrations were not what she was searching for. She had no patience and was not prepared to spend any time talking with them. If I were to persevere with taking a couple of hours 'my time' then I would have to cope with the repercussions. The best way forward seemed to be for me to devote my entire time to caring for Bet – and to try to keep us on a level calm pathway. Friends were obviously concerned for my welfare and I am not sure that they understood why I chose not to search out more respite care. In the long term it was the easiest pathway.

We took daily short walks. Initially we would cross the road from the flat, walk a couple of hundred yards, and enter Fox Rosehill Gardens – quite a magic collection of tropical and sub-tropical plants. We could never stay long – for Bet would 'need a wee' and a refill of her water bottle. After a few of these journeys Bet realised that even the couple of hundred yards was too much. There were falls and she needed my arm for support. There were times, however, when her need to assert her independence seemed to enable her to achieve incredible physical stamina. In July we went, with Ann and Kevin, to visit Paul's farm over at Manaccan. Paul was our 'daffodil man' in early spring – and in the summer he supplied us with local honey. We walked around his fields – over a mile probably – and Bet insisted on making her own way, without any help. I could tell the supreme effort that she was making. She was determined to appear strong. She never wanted to accept that she had a problem. She fought against my decision to buy a wheel chair. She hated the idea and I can totally understand why.

By September Bet's ability to walk had continued to deteriorate. Our daily walk from the flat was now just a couple of hundred yards along the level roadway where we would peep through a gate, always locked, into the lush garden of the neighbouring block of flats. This became our 'secret garden' – just a few minutes walk away but still with Bet clutching a bottle of water in her 'good hand' and her weak arm firmly linked through mine. Ann and Kevin continued to help to try to maintain our lives 'as normal' and we arranged a visit to the Eden Project. This was an hour's drive and we would certainly need the wheelchair. Bet had fears but accepted that this would be a good day out!

It was quite a long way but we got there without a problem. My chair was useful because there was a toilet wherever I went...
Bet Kaye 18th September 2014

This was interesting. We didn't need to stop en route. There was no call for 'a wee'. Bet accepted leaving the car and getting into her chair without any problem. However, from that point onwards, she demanded the toilet wherever we went. Not only did I have to wheel her to every disabled toilet on the site – but also I had to wheel her into the cabin, twisting and manoeuvring. She certainly could easily have got out of her chair and walked into the toilet – but that was not what she was about. It was almost as though she was determined to make it as difficult as she possibly could for me. I had insisted on her having the chair – so she would get back at me in this way! It probably wasn't malicious in intent – or was it? For the two years that I cared for Bet I could never distinguish how she might be feeling.

The day after our Eden adventure I took Bet to see a chiropractor. I talked with him prior to our visit and asked him to explain to Bet how her difficulties couldn't be sorted in the way that she hoped. We had already had 'healing sessions' of various kinds and my NHS team were worried that this was money being 'thrown away'. Another dilemma I had to try to sort out for I knew how much faith Bet set on 'alternative therapies'. Was it better to continue to allow her this treatment? The alternative seemed too stark a reality and I didn't want to let Bet down in this way. This lovely chiropractor explained very gently the limitations of any treatment he could offer. As we left Bet was silent. She must have felt very distressed but she didn't show it. Her diary entry, very untidily written, simply states:

> *Then after some psyllium husks we went to see the chiropractor who couldn't do the job. Now it's lunchtime and I'll eat my dinner with water between every mouthful...*
> *Bet Kaye 19th September 2014*

It would be several days before her diary indicated that she needed to see another chiropractor. From that point on we would reassure her that we were continuing to search for the right one. The one with the 'magic wand'!

In August Sam and I had organised a surprise gathering for Bet's 70th birthday. We gathered an eclectic collection of friends from Falmouth and from Altarnun and beyond. Bet seemed to understand what was happening and appeared pleased that so many friends were there. However, her diary entry is curiously very mundane:

> *We got ready to go out for a meal. I couldn't believe what happened. We had a lovely meal. It was mackerel pate (with no bones). It was very posh and Ian took lots of photos. The pork had a huge amount of veg to eat and ended with Eton Mess. Maggie kept giving me*

her fruit salad. There were lots of people there even Richard Herring. Pat and Ken were there. Donna. And Andy's stopped smoking. I'm pleased about that.
Bet Kaye 17th August 2014

There is no mention, for example, about all the lovely flowers she received, and lots of gifts. Peter had painted her portrait and had sent it from the Isle of Wight. We opened it in front of all the guests. Bet looked at it and said "That's fine – although it doesn't look like me!" That was the end of that! All we could do was to hope that in some way Bet had been pleased and that she would have realised that she was surrounded by people who cared for her – and loved her.

It was 5th September when I was summoned to Treliske Hospital for my TURPs! – the Transurethral Resection of the Prostate. The medical team scheduled me for a Friday to make it easier for Sam to look after her mum, for I would have to stay in hospital for 24 hours at least. The Patient Information sheet makes it all sound so straightforward and I was not going to be over anxious about 'spinal anaesthetic' or even the 'telescopic instrument called a cystoscope ' which would be passed 'along the urethra to your prostate'. However had it read that it was 'a tube pushed right up through your penis' – then I might have felt a little apprehensive. As it was I was determined to watch every thing in detail. This was a new experience and I would make the most of it. And I was having a weekend away from home. This was a holiday! I watched the procedure on a screen – and was fascinated by the mesmerising sight as all the flakes were scalped off my diseased prostate gland. Even the thought of having a catheter inserted was reassuring. I would have a night without having to get up every hour. Bet wasn't the only one with a sensitive bladder! I actually managed two nights in hospital and returned home minus catheter on the Sunday.

My holiday was over. Bet showed little concern for the fact that I needed rest. It was back to the routine and the daily meals and walks. What I didn't anticipate was the pain I would now have to suffer whenever I needed 'a wee'! This was a week of agony – the cut glass syndrome! It gradually eased and the flow was better. My nights were still broken – but I began to sleep for longer spells. Thankfully at this stage Bet's bladder was quiet and content during the nights. And she was able to go to the toilet without my help. In fact, looking back over a year ago – I had it rather easy!

As soon as we had sold Arwenack Avenue and moved into a rented flat I realised that I would be liable for paying for Bet's care – and that this need would grow. I would have to buy another home. The alternative would be to watch our saving's account dwindle – perhaps to the extent that we would never be able to afford to buy a property again. These are the financial practicalities which all carers have to face, additional worries and anxieties at a time when life can seem tough enough. We went to look at a brand new bungalow out on the edge of town. It was a small development of properties especially designed for wheelchair use. It was a lovely bungalow, beautifully designed within grounds which would be maintained. There was no way I could cope with gardening at this stage! The bungalow did have a lovely outside decked area; it boasted under floor heating, and had a wet room as well as an en suite to the larger of the two bedrooms. It was ideal. The only disadvantage was that it was a couple of miles out of town. Bet had reached a stage where we had to use the car to travel anywhere – so I reasoned that an extra couple of miles were a small price to pay. Bet never warmed to the place however. She felt it was too far from Sam's house. She was determined that she would never really like it. It would make our lives easier and so I made the decision to buy. We would move in on 22nd October and my radiotherapy would begin during November. We would have to give serious thought to where Bet could go whilst my daily treatment took place.

Bet spent the removal day with Maggie. That evening Wendy and Gordon brought a meal around which was a very thoughtful idea. At 6pm they rang to ask if I could find a pan? I managed to find a box labelled 'kitchen' and was pleased to pull out a pan. The hotplate was more of a challenge. I had never had a touch screen for my pans before! But I discovered heat! Half an hour later and Gordon rang again. This time he asked if I could put the oven on! Heck! This was serious stuff! The manual was pages thick and the multi function spaceship didn't look as though it would ever lift off! It did and we managed to find the table and four chairs. Typically Becca's Kev arrived a day late to help me move – but that was very useful.

I needed to return to the flat and make sure it was clear and clean. Around teatime I returned to the bungalow to find Kev very concerned. He had found Bet unconscious on the kitchen floor. She had quickly recovered and could stand. Her walking, however, seemed very uncoordinated and he was worried. She seemed confused – more than usual. She now seemed unable to stand without our help. I rang our GP who suggested that we should call an ambulance. The team arrived quite quickly and helped Bet onto the bed where the paramedic gave her an examination. When asked her name she said "Betty Dowse" – back to her maiden name. We obviously went through her behaviour patterns and when we came to the over-dosing of water intake the paramedic felt that was the key! Bet was now going into a very sleepy state and seemed to be losing what little hold she had on the reality around her. Off they took her to hospital with me following behind in the car. Haunted by memories of the many times I had driven behind the ambulance carrying our daughter I felt numb. What was happening? Could I cope?

The ambulance team met me as I arrived at A&E and showed me to the bay where Bet lay almost asleep. She was calm and already coupled up to monitors. A nurse reassured me that a doctor would be with us shortly. Eventually a junior doctor did pull herself away from the computer screen and her bottle of squash – unaware that I had been watching her messing around for the past ten minutes. She came in and began to ask me questions. Suddenly Bet went into a severe seizure. An alarm rang and a senior doctor rushed in and took control. They now realised that Bet's condition was serious. There were a series of injections and more tubes were added. Science was now taking control of Bet's body. A good job she was oblivious!

Eventually we were moved into a darkened area where there were silent bodies surrounded by technology. Numbers and graphs on lighted screens; gentle beeping reassuring us that life was still present; and the awful clang of the metal waste bin! Surely, in this arena of the latest science, someone could design a silent rubbish bin? I was taken out and into a small lounge area where a doctor came to talk to me. I was prepared I suppose. I had experienced these chats about death before and the routine doesn't really change. I found myself comparing the dialogue with past experience – with the doctors who would talk to us about Bet's dad, my own father and with Becca – several times with her! She was such a fighter! Now I was being told that Bet could die. She was very ill. A decision would be made as to whether or not she would be resuscitated if she was to suffer heart failure and all would be done to avoid pain and unnecessary stress. The doctor told me that he would leave me to telephone Sam. At that point the reality set in. I would now have to verbalise the experience of the past few hours. For a brief moment I felt helpless. I just stared at my phone. It rang! It was Sam. She had come to find us and was now outside A&E. I was so pleased to have her by my side.

Bet was moved into a side ward during the night and we continued to sit by her side. They brought us sandwiches and looked after us. I had an appointment with the radiotherapy team at 9am and so I left Sam with her mum and headed for the Sunrise Centre and my rendezvous with the nuclear beams. I was to be measured and tattooed. I must have looked a very dishevelled sight – even for that team who are used to dealing with the worst that cancer can throw at folk. They were very understanding and comforting but despite all the love, which I felt around me, I couldn't get my bladder to the state it needed to be! My body was totally dehydrated and I suppose I was knackered! Another appointment was given me for a few days later. My bladder was the problem!

Both of us were in hospital! Both of us by courtesy of our bladders!

"Miranda was funny – which is more than I can say for Peter!"

Monday 2nd November 2015

I am driving into Truro today and have Shirley with me. I know I should be clambering up the hill and sweating off the kilos, for I had blood tests this morning to check my PSA and my blood-sugar level, but the company is reassuring. Shirley's husband Ken is in the room opposite to Bet's, and as I pass by their home if I am driving, it is a great help to us both to cope with the long corridor together. We are both tired and wearied by years of caring. Neither of us knows how much longer we will make these daily journeys and both of us will feel guilty as we inevitably sometimes wish that our partner's suffering would come to a peaceful end.

Shirley's husband is in the dining room and so we part company. I find Bet sitting in her chair. The television is on but I am aware that she pays little attention to it. Her eyesight seems to be failing. She allows me to change to a radio station and 'Magic Radio' is her choice today. It still concerns me that those who care for patients with dementia do not always appreciate how stimulating music can be. Bet loves her music.

A year previously we had prepared ourselves for the fact that Bet might die. She recovered and was eventually moved back into the local hospital in Falmouth. At the same time my body had allowed itself to be measured up for radiotherapy and the relevant tattoo marks etched on my then rather podgy tummy. The pressure was on – for there were 37 sessions to fit in and we were already going to run over Christmas and into the New Year. The team in the aptly named 'Sunrise Centre' were so patient with me. They already seemed such good friends. I felt that I could trust them and that they would do their best to cure me.

We had to find residential care for Bet as a matter of urgency, and this proved problematic. According to our psychiatric 'support team' there wasn't a single bed available for 'respite care' in the whole of Cornwall. I felt that I had to do something myself. 'Crossroads' had told me that if I ever needed help then I must go and see them. I needed help. Bet was ready to be discharged from hospital and my treatment had to commence. 'Crossroads' was full – but the Manager agreed to find Bet a room. Bless them! I thought that Bet would be happy to return there. I collected her from hospital and drove her over to 'Crossroads'. Although she seemed happy to meet with the staff, she was initially confused by the fact that she now had a different room. And having suffered from excessive liquid intake the medical advice was that she couldn't have a cup of tea whenever she wanted. Someone else would now have to battle with her. They too would suffer her wrath! She was not happy there and always pleased when I collected her on a Friday afternoon and drove her home. Taking her back there on a Sunday afternoon was never easy!

I now had to focus on my own treatment. I had been diagnosed with a fairly aggressive prostate cancer, locally advanced, and with a Gleason score of 9! I really hadn't had the time to be worried and I attended my daily sessions with what must, to other patients, have appeared a carefree heart. It wasn't easy! I affectionately referred to the experience as 'bladder torture'. My bladder had to be 'as close to bursting as possible' before treatment would commence. This was to avoid damaging adjacent bladder and bowel tissues and maximising the intensity of the beams on the cancer cells. The routine became common. I would be called over the tannoy system and the other patients would look up hoping to see that young chubby Lancashire comedian who has taken my name. My smiling treatment team would ask me if my bladder was 'bursting'. In the early days I would think it was and would go forward into the futuristic inner sanctum, lie on the specially measured couch with my tattoos accurately lined up. The machine would take over as my team left me to watch my bladder on their screen. The machine would raise me and then surround me. Above was the impression of a roof light, blossom on a tree and a sunlit blue sky above. This was a peaceful few moments. If my bladder was 'full to bursting' then I would hear a click and the machine would begin the serious part of the treatment and I would visualise the cancer cells shrivelling under the powerful radioactive beams.

Sadly this rarely happened. Instead of the reassuring 'click' I would hear footsteps hurrying up the corridor and the heavy door being opened.

"Sorry Peter! Nowhere near full enough!" one of the team would say with a huge smile.

They would lower me down and help me off the couch. I would struggle back into my trousers and shoes feeling that they must be wrong! I would apologise and they would reassure me and tell me not to worry. I was not alone, they would try to convince me, and such false starts were built into the system. I would have to return to the waiting room and drink a further half litre of water. Occasionally I would have a second false start – and then I would really get upset. The only way, and it could take me up to two hours and two litres of water, was to aim for a point so close to wetting myself that once I did! I came to the conclusion that the hormone treatment I was having, an injection once every three months, was leading to hot flushes. I was perhaps dehydrated. Yes this was my 'bladder torture' and I will be ever grateful to the young ladies who laughed with me and supported me throughout the experience. Sometimes Sam would drive me to the hospital and then go on and visit her mother. On days where I drove myself in for treatment I would go and visit Bet myself. She was continuing to keep her diary and it reveals that she still failed to appreciate the nature of my problem.

Dad is in hospital with his impacted stomach. Don't know if he's having more scans. He seems to spend a

*lot of time with doctors. I saw him first thing and then
I heard his voice tonight.*
Bet Kaye 3rd November 2014

*Everyone is very supportive here and I am drinking
as much water as I dare. I keep hearing Ian B asking
where I am...*
Bet Kaye 6th November 2014

This last entry was on my birthday and there is a passing mention of lunch out with Sam and myself. The 'voices' are still there as is the hope that Ian B will still whisk her away! It is also interesting to note that she sees the limitation of her water as an imposition that she will try to overcome. There was never any understanding of the serious nature of her admission to hospital. In fact she soon appears to have forgotten that it happened. From this point onwards her diary entries become much more intermittent and her handwriting is weaker as she struggles to hold her pen. There is reference to food but never to my visits. There is also a growing tendency to include such detail as '*I did three good poos*'.

Weekends should have been good. We had our new bungalow and I was being treated by the full resources of the NHS, the very latest in technology and daily bouts of fun and laughter from such a caring radiotherapy team. Why was it that I seemed incapable of making this happiness continue into the weekends? Why was I beginning to dread my role as a 'carer'? I began to suspect that I was no longer capable. Perhaps this was a result of my own illness? Perhaps the effects of daily blasts of radiotherapy? Sam and I began to explore the idea that we would find a permanent residential care home – preferably in Falmouth. We approached Treverne, which we knew had a long waiting list. We looked around and it appeared clean and well organised. We asked for Bet to be placed on the waiting list. The home was just a few hundred yards from Sam's home and just across the road from the flat we had rented in the summer. I felt a sense of elation. It would be so easy to visit her every day, to take her out for walks and for friends to call in whenever they were nearby. We were told that there would need to be a 'top up fee' paid by us and I accepted that this would be necessary. At that point I knew no different.

A few weeks later Treverne let us know that an ensuite room had become available in the new wing. It would be available before Christmas and we arranged to transfer Bet on 16th December. She seemed to understand that this would be so much more convenient for us all. That day would be particularly appropriate for in the afternoon the home was hosting a local primary school choir with Christmas songs and in the evening the Salvation Army was scheduled to be playing carols. This would thrill Bet and certainly make her feel at home and cared for. Although I made it very clear to the staff that music was so important to Bet – she was not taken to either of the events. I was bitterly disappointed. It may not have been the staff's fault. They may have asked her and she may have refused. They claimed that they wanted to leave her in her room so that she would settle. It was not a good start. And it went from bad to worse.

I collected Bet on the following Friday afternoon and then returned her on Sunday evening. She was not happy and struggled when I tried to help her from the car. I reassured her that in three day's time I would be collecting her for Christmas. I had treatment on Christmas Eve and then four days off. I would try my best to make Christmas happy for us all. The tree was up and the lights were on.

Bet, however, refused to be happy. I was constantly reminded that our psychiatrist Dr K had once told me that Bet would never be happy wherever she was. I suppose the medical people were preparing me for the time when I would have to place Bet permanently into care. I still believed that I could bring laughter back into our lives. I don't think I fully appreciated that I, myself, had stopped smiling when I was with Bet. She noticed and must have felt distressed by my obvious discomfort.

> *...and now it is 'Miranda' which is very amusing - which is more than I can say for Peter! ...What a miserable place this is. I wish we lived nearer town... Bet Kaye Christmas Eve 2014*

Sam and I did our best but we knew that Christmas would never be the same. We both remembered our family gatherings, where Herbie had arrived with a gigantic turkey and all the family had pulled crackers and donned paper hats. Rylands had been a particularly magical place at Christmas time. The small cosy cottage rooms, with their low beams and stone walls, seemed comforting; the family were all within such easy reach across the courtyard; we were isolated from the world and surrounded by evergreen trees, and, above all, Bet was holding us all together – the central maternal figure in her tiny but ever so efficient kitchen. And there would be music! Becca would sort out the 'entertainment' and Sam would be the strong supporting act!

We had moved to Rylands in 1984. The move didn't go to plan. Having decided that we would ask our parents to move down with us we were faced with two major problems. The first was to find suitable accommodation for us all. Hmm! The second was to sell three separate homes in Scarborough in order to buy in Cornwall. Hmm! And so I drove down to Cornwall with Sam and Becca for the start of our new school year. A well-meaning school governor had found us a 'suitable flat' for the three of us. The three tired travellers pulled into a muddy farmyard, way out in the rural wilds beyond the Tamar, and our hearts sank. Heaven knows what my children must have thought. I had dragged them from one side of the country to the other, away from their friends, their mum and their cat! And now we fiddled with a reluctant key to the sound and smells of the pigs in the adjacent sties, before having to come to terms with the reality of a 'local one up and one down for local people' and the fact that we no longer had a microwave, double glazing, central heating or even a bed to call our own. The girls had to share an ancient double bed where springs could be easily counted and would play tunes throughout the night. I had the luxury of the downstairs settee, which was possibly slightly more comfortable if less exciting.

I'm not sure our first days in Launceston College were any less of a challenge. Sam was heart-broken when on her first day her English teacher gave her a red '0/10' as she had produced a beautiful poem and delightfully illustrated it over a double page. Apparently her teacher had told the class to write the poem on the 'first page'. As her poem was too long to fit on the first single page I had suggested that she turned over and used the double page. Sam was heart-broken. I was livid and thrown into a terrible dilemma. The teacher happened to be the Head of the English Department and I, as the new Deputy Head, could hardly complain about my own child's treatment on my first day. I did! As tactfully as I could. But the harm had been done and Sam, already lacking in self-confidence, disliked the man from that point onwards. As I constructed the school's timetable I was able to avoid the pair ever meeting again in future years. Sadly it took us many years before we were able to remove such an insensitive teacher from the classroom.

Most of the teachers, as you would expect, were thoughtful and kind. The Home Economics Department were particularly helpful. In those days 'Cookery' was high on the agenda and rightly so.

Almost every evening we would bring home a 'quiche', a flan or a savoury tart of some description – usually made by some poor student who lacked the money or the drive to provide the necessary ingredients and had been given them by the school. It was better not to ask who had made the offering!

We had a date fixed for 'completion' for our house sale and we were so disappointed when it fell through at the very last moment. Apparently the lady had a change of heart as she picked up the pen to sign in the solicitor's office. You can't get closer than that! After months of expectancy all hopes were now shattered and we were back to the beginning. Happily my mum's bungalow was having better luck as was Bet's parents home. Bet had remained in Scarborough calmly coordinating what must have been, in anyone else's mind, a nightmare. She came down for a weekend and we were thrilled – if even more crowded in our rural pad!

It all fell into place after a couple of months and the commune came together. The furniture van did get caught in the branches of a tree as it edged its way down the narrow lane to Rylands but luckily Bet's dad had a saw handy in the back of his car. Walt clambered up into the hedge and removed the culprit! This would be our life style now for the next twenty years. Our numbers would decrease as the elders passed away and the children moved on to university but they would increase again as 'Rylands' morphed into holiday lets and rejoiced again as children returned, and then left, and then returned again. Throughout the pulsating years Bet would keep it all together responding to each stage with a calmness that exuded love. Little wonder that over the past year Bet would frequently chant out "Half my heart will always be at Rylands".

Another frequent statement during Bet's illness has been, "And I looked after our children and our parents. That seemed to be the most important thing!" She would adamantly and vehemently claim this whenever visitors arrived, as though searching back to a time when she was able to influence our lives. It was as though she was defending herself against the realisation that now she was weak and physically helpless. No one could disagree with her. Her contribution to our extended family had been paramount and crucial. She had cared for us all.

She loved our Rylands' garden. Immediately she set to work with her Dad. Walt, retired now from farming, but still a farmer at heart, loved being with his 'little girl' again. They arranged for the paddock to be ploughed over, much to Sam's chagrin as she had hoped for a pony, and it was soon planted up with potatoes. That was just the start. The garden was just under an acre in total but divided into many small sections, which made it a fascinating place to wander through and round. My mother came to love it too – which compensated for her initial disappointment when she first entered her cottage, looked disparagingly around, and uttered, "This is not what I'm used to!"

I think we were all a little disappointed by the

reality. Rylands was externally a 'chocolate box cottage' but now, living inside, we came to appreciate that there were problems. Winter was approaching, and although the climate was a whole top coat warmer in Cornwall than on the exposed North Yorkshire coast, the cottages had neither central heating, nor double glazing and the odd, ancient night store heaters were expensive to run. The beams seemed to be a mass of woodworm holes and the floorboards bounced in our freezing bedrooms. We soon began to improve things thanks to the financial input from our elders, for my mother was certainly not going to put up with draughty windows for long!

There were two problems with the property that would seem to have been beyond even the finances of our combined pockets. The roof of the original cottage was severely 'sagging' and although this gave Rylands an additional quaintness it was rather a worrying weakness. The second 'problem' was the state of the electrical circuits – although circuits is probably far too modern a term to apply to the myriad crocheting collection of archaic wiring which seemed to be hidden behind every cobwebbed corner. In one highly dangerous manoeuvre I managed to solve both deficiencies. I had found a spare, potentially 'live wire' and coupled it onto a new extractor fan in Walt's kitchen. Later that evening a car pulled to a halt and neighbours asked if we were aware that smoke was pothering out of the roof above Walter's flat. In that ceiling void was Bet's store of fabrics. These were now smouldering away lying innocently above an ancient wire, which had recently been brought to life! Waiting for the fire brigade to navigate the country lanes and hearing them stop at every tiny junction is not an activity I would recommend to the feint hearted. They did arrive eventually and immediately asked us where there was a hydrant. Oh well! There was a river nearby if the worst came to the worst. We directed them to the room above and told them that the smouldering storeroom was at the far side, along past Sam's six foot snooker table!

"'Ere lads! There's a pool table! You take care now!" shouted the broad Cornish accent at the two brave souls who had donned breathing apparatus and were heading up the stairs with their axes at the ready. I think it would have remained a fairly contented smouldering heap if our two courageous lads had not yanked open the store door and blessed the dormant fire with a massive burst of good old Cornish air! Ooops! The little man on the ladder outside went into action and ripped away the slates. Nothing like adding a bit more fuel to the fire! For a brief moment gigantic and hungry flames burst into the air and we thought that that was the end of our Rylands' dream. Within a minute the flames were out, but not before water had flooded down into Walt and Con's home. When we went up into the loft area we were saddened to realise how much damage smoke and water could cause. The computer was destroyed – as were all my OU books and essays. We had lost many photographs. Furniture too would have to be written off and replaced. But one thing had survived. Before they had tackled the awaiting blaze, the firemen, communicating in signs, had lifted Sam's snooker table, and turned it over carefully onto the bed. Apart from one tiny speck of soot on one corner pocket the 'pool table' had been saved. These Cornish lads certainly have clear priorities!

And so, a few months later, Rylands boasted a new roof and a brand new electric circuit. This is not a technique I would recommend for it took us months to rid our homes of the smell of smoke and our minds of the utter helplessness we all felt as we realised how lucky we had all been. If only I could have found a solution to the septic tank! That damned contraption was neatly packaged in a parcel of land over the lane. In theory it was 'out of sight and out of mind'. It was part of Farmer Burford's field which gently sloped down to a stream. Cows grazed there and the septic tank bubbled and gurgled in rural harmony. That was until Farmer Burford decided that there was far more profit to be made by planting young saplings than by selling milk. It was an easier life style too. The only problem was that within a couple of years the root systems of the growing forest were to play nasty tricks on the drainage and our septic tank would no longer function! I would spend hours during school holidays, digging until I was waste deep in trenches, in some vain attempt to clear our clogged drains. Eventually we had to pay the digger man a fortune and gain ourselves a further couple of years without a backlog of sewage! I am not sure I remember Rylands with the same fondness as does Bet!

She continued to thrive! With her Dad by her side the harvests would be gathered and the surplus vegetables and fruits sold off in Richard's shop – the central hub of Altarnun village. In many ways we became almost self sufficient and Bet was in her element. She also began to teach again with just a few hours each week in a couple of local primary schools. She worked with individual children, helping them with basic skills in number and language. Her work was much appreciated, both by the schools and by the children themselves, and she could have easily gained more hours each week. However her priorities were firmly rooted in the Rylands' community and she continued to be available whenever the extended family needed her help. My mum didn't drive so Bet would take her shopping; my sister Pauline began to attend sessions in a nearby care home and Bet would make sure that she was always delivered safely. She supported her dad as he cared for her mum. Con had been diagnosed with Multiple Sclerosis, we think as a result of crop spraying above their Lincolnshire farm many years previously, and was now using a wheel chair. And together we ferried our growing children as they developed their interests. Sam's journeys took us backwards and forwards to Mandy's stables for further lessons in riding, mucking out and swearing, then on to gymkhanas and onwards to A&E! Never a dull moment! Becca, on the other hand, should have proved easier on the nerves, except that her clarinet lessons took place on the other side of Bodmin Moor. Not easy in winter!

I will never forget the first snow of our first winter. I happened to be 'in charge' of the school as the Head was out. It was lunch time and I noted a few tiny specks of snow floating harmlessly downwards from a rather grey sky. There was just a hint, on the grass, that a thin coat might settle. The phone rang in my office. It was the Secretary.

"Ere luver! You goin' to close the school?"

"No. Why?" I was puzzled.

"Tis snowing! You look you out of your window!" she continues in her lovely Cornish maid's accent.

"Get on! You're joking!" I retaliated with the thickest Barnsley accent I could remember. "You dun't know what snow is! We're ah cum frum we 'as snow rate up to are bottoms and beyond! This in't snow! It's fairy dust!"

"Well we think the school should be closed. Now!" and she slammed down the phone. I couldn't believe this conversation. My mind went back to Scarborough where I remembered loading children onto a school bus and having to shovel snow out of the doorway before it could slide its way forward through the blizzard. Twenty minutes later and the phone blared out again.

"We've had Webber's on and they are sending in their buses now. If you don't close the school they won't collect the children later! You have got to close the school!"

I looked out of my window. The buses were piling into the coach park. The snow was still gently falling and the grass now did look white. We closed the school and all the children and staff got home safely. The next morning Radio Cornwall announced that all Cornish schools were closed for the day and Rylands was a magical scene. That morning Bet and I walked the half mile to the village, our footsteps marking the virgin snow and the sound of silence filling our hearts and minds. I reflected on how close I had come to having a disaster on my hands. The Moor is a myriad of tiny hamlets linked together by the narrowest of lanes and hills. An inch of snow can bring a school bus to a stand still miles from anywhere and rescue would be difficult. Some of our pupils travelled for two hours to get to school – and that's two hours to get home on a dark winter's night! I didn't forget. Not that I ever had that situation again. It doesn't snow very often in Cornwall.

As the elders became more reliant on Bet's help she would calmly sort them out. Con eventually had to go into hospital and shortly after, whilst playing bowls in Wadebridge, her dad suffered a heart attack from which he was never to recover. Bet felt that he had died of a broken heart. I think her heart was broken too! She really did love her Dad so much. From this point on I would have to help more with the garden! I enjoyed certain things. Cutting the lawns could take me up to five hours. I planned my lessons that way! Bet now spent more time sewing. She had continued to develop her puppets and she had little outlets for her badgers and foxes throughout North Cornwall. One year a friend, who had a stall selling her patchwork at The Royal Cornwall Show, asked if she could sell some of Bet's puppets. Every night there would be a frantic phone call to ask if we could rush over further supplies – and from that point on we knew that Bet's puppets were being loved! The following year Bet had her own stall in the craft marquee at The Royal Cornwall Show. "Bit's O' Fluff" were firmly on the road!

I look across from the side of Bet's bed and there is one of our favourites. The 'otter'! The otter came with her to Kenwyn and will stay with her forever. It is such a lovely creation. I don't think Shirley has seen it in action. I go over and go straight into autopilot – demonstration mode. I animate the creature and bring it alive, carefully carrying it into Ken's room. Shirley is suitably impressed, initially thinking I had a real animal in my arms. I go back and tell Bet. I hope she understands. I hope she can still appreciate the magic she created and the joy she brought to thousands of children – of all ages!

One of the rare occasions I find myself smiling!

"What's the name of that village?"

Sunday 8ᵗʰ November 2015

B et is cradled in her bed. She looks well cared for, with a nest of spotlessly clean pillows snuggled around her. The chart shows that she is being turned every two hours.

Two days ago I reached the age of 72. The age itself is meaningless and I am just grateful that I have survived long enough to make sure that Bet is as comfortable as she can be. Joan and Peter are with me today and are chatting to Bet and she is responding calmly and with a degree of interest. She has a little of the strawberries and yoghurt – but no more than a few teaspoons. I clean her teeth and moisten her lips and she has a few sips of tea that gurgle in her throat. Then I read a little more of "Why the Whales Came" the second Michael Morpurgo book, which Katie has selected for us. My friends know that this is probably the last time they will see Bet and I am so grateful that they are prepared to sit with us now and share that experience.

Joan and Peter travelled down from the Isle of Wight and arrived Thursday evening. They are staying with me until tomorrow and have been in to Kenwyn every day to talk to Bet and to support me. Last night four friends invited us to a newly opened Italian restaurant to celebrate my birthday. Joan was angry that my friends never mentioned Bet throughout the two hours of the meal. Such avoidance seems usual with my closest friends in Falmouth. Whether they are afraid of upsetting me, or distressing themselves, I do not know. As a society we don't seem particularly good at talking about serious illness and death. I know if I were to ask any of my friends for help they would do so – and willingly. I rarely ask though. Joan, on the other hand, never waits to be asked. She is a forthright organiser, and for that, I am grateful. I am so tired of making lonely decisions.

Sam and I had hoped that by moving Bet into Treverne, in the middle of Falmouth, our friends would call in and visit. Only Maggie made the effort. I know it was not easy. Bet's behaviour was strange and it was difficult to make conversation or avoid being kicked. But she did know her 'friends' and did appreciate when they came to visit. And it certainly would have helped me. I know that visiting a dementia unit can be a disturbing experience for some people but illness and death, are, for heaven's sake, integral parts of our lives. We cannot simply ignore such things. Some people do though. They prefer not to think about such 'distressing happenings' until they have to meet them head on. Too late then to formulate any plans, for the treadmill will have already started to turn.

Even if friends had visited Bet every day she would still have been unhappy. I know that. I know that only I could make the decision about the way forward and I remember how difficult it was. The only way I could have contemplated leaving Bet in

Treverne (or any care home) at that stage would have been for me to turn my back and never visit her again. I know I had to 'rescue' her from Treverne. This was not the right environment for her. She had far too much awareness to be in a 'dementia unit' and was often in tears. She was once knocked to the ground by another resident and her body badly bruised. The only possible solution was to complete my radiotherapy, have a few days break and then take her home. That was my purpose. What else could I do with my life? Sam would be close by and hopefully Bet would begin to accept more help being introduced into our home. I worked out all the positives. I had survived the past two months of 'bladder torture' and I could be a reasonably good carer! Super carer even! Every minute of every day someone is facing the same dilemma. There is no right or wrong. I would follow my heart – no heroics – that's just the way I am.

And typically I landed with a massive thwack! Bet had now started to lash out both physically and verbally. I had bought her a new diary for Christmas and when she came home she made an effort to scribble in entries

...the sun is shining to welcome me home. I'm so glad
I am back – nobody to talk to, but at least I have left.
Thank goodness!
Bet Kaye 16th January 2015

I've watched so much bloody telly like I did in Treverne.
So glad I have escaped...
Bet Kaye 17th January 2015

I managed a second poo today which made me comfortable. I am hoping Sam will come soon otherwise we'll have been watching telly all night.
Bet Kaye 19th January 2015

Now Pete is faffing around and I need my eyes testing. We've watch two films today. It's as bad as Treverne...
Bet Kaye 20th January 2015

Woke up early and had an exceptionally good poo. Bugger off. Debbie came and we chatted quite a lot.
Bet Kaye 29th January 2015

We went to Mawnan Smith and then to Budock. We went all round the houses. We went to Constantine this afternoon. We saw a dead badger on the road. We've just had a meal and I've had another poo...
Bet Kaye 3rd February 2015

The frustrations are evident even within Bet's minimal scribbles. Although she 'hated' Treverne, she was far from happy at home. A routine was soon established. Bet could manage to walk slowly from her bed into her en suite toilet. She had control of her bodily functions and her diary makes this point clearly. Everything else she had had to delegate to me. I then helped her into the wet room where we would shower together. It was at this stage that she began to whack me in the groin. Was this playful or malicious? I know initially it upset me – and I should have known better! It would have been so much easier if I could just have accepted it, laughed, and moved on. Instead I tried to reason with her. I would ask her to explain why she was wanting to hurt me but there was no understanding of my 'hurt'. Even when she would bite my shoulder, often leaving teeth marks, it was, to her, just a kiss. Or was it?

After a shower, where she would always ask me to wash her hair, I had to dry her, dress her and then position her in front of the mirror and begin the ten minutes of directed styling with the 'hot brush' or whatever the hot prongy thing was called. I had to begin in the correct place and not move on until I was sure that section was dry. At the end she would violently take her hair brush and even more angrily maul through my work. My very best efforts would gain an 'It'll do!" More often than not I would be aiding her towards the breakfast table fending off grumbles and thumps.

Breakfast was never an easy meal for she would demand her three courses – fruit and yoghurt, followed by porridge and finally a slice of toast dripping with marmite – and I am one of those people who cannot stand even the smell of the stuff! As well as keeping the flow of food consistent I had to manoeuvre in a goodly concoction of tablets. Some were accepted but others, after discovering them hidden or thrown onto the kitchen floor, I would have to grind up and add to the fruit and yoghurt. As soon as food had been devoured then Bet struggled to her feet and I would have to take her back to the bathroom to clean her teeth. Thankfully she would then want to sit down and ask me to turn on the television. Only then could I begin to find my own breakfast.

Although her diary entries suggest that she doesn't really want to watch television, this is always what she asked to do. I am now an expert in daytime TV! And in the evening she would be adamant that she needed to watch the 'soaps'. She returned from Treverne where she had watched her television, it would seem, for most of the day, addicted to the 'everyday life' of murder, disaster, rape and pillage. At least 'Crossroads' had hosted a variety of afternoon activities and encouraged clients out of their rooms, I am not sure that Treverne was as proactive. Bet and I, had never watched 'East Enders' or 'Coronation Street' for years – and I don't think I had ever seen a single episode of 'Emmerdale' until Bet now claimed to be following all the stories with interest and concern. In reality she wasn't really aware of the story lines and, if questioned, couldn't distinguish one programme from another. But her routine did allow me to sit down and gain a little respite. It is so important to search out the positives!

I did try to add other activities into our days. I returned to our crossword puzzles, but soon discovered that Bet was no longer the quick-witted person she had been even six months earlier. She now would show some frustration and claim that I had always been more intelligent than she had been. Not true of course, and I would try to reassure her, but she knew that she was failing. Her anger with me would appear as a cover. One thing she did enjoy was to get into our car and allow me to drive her gently around the local villages. She particularly liked driving through Mawnan Smith for some reason. It has a small village square and I would drive her into the car park there. We never stayed long. We would have to get back before the need for the toilet became a problem. Even when we were invited to a neighbour's house for a 'cup of tea' Bet would ask to use the loo as soon as we had arrived.

We went to Ulla's this afternoon. I managed two wees
Bet Kaye 19th January 2015

She was still hoping for a chiropractor who could cure her.

I need a bloody chiropractor. This afternoon we've been out for a nice drive round the point. It's been a miserable old day. Not much else to say...
Bet Kaye 21st January 2015

Strangely Bet never forgot the word 'chiropractor'. As time went on she would struggle to remember various words or places. She had decided that the Duchy Hospital, Cornwall's private hospital, was a place where she could be cured. "Duchy, Duchy, Duchy!" she would often sing but would then, moments later, forget its name.

"What's the name of that hospital?", she would often ask, before going into another musical rendition.

It was about this time that she began to talk about 'Herbie'. Now Herb is another friend who probably finds it impossible to be close to death and suffering. In fact Herbie disappeared from our lives after Becca died. I had met Herb in 1965 when we both found ourselves as Volunteer Teachers sharing a three day orienteering session in Kuching, the capital of Sarawak. Herb and I had gone out for a walk through the town. We were both tall and sporting long white legs. The natives stared at us with a degree of polite amusement. We each bought a wide brimmed rattan hat to protect ourselves from the sun. Instantly we began to make friends. Children surrounded us. There was laughter as they followed us along the narrow streets and through the open market.

"What a wonderful country!" we remarked. "What friendly people!" Only later did we discover that we had bought women's hats – the sort only worn in the rice paddies! Oh we had made a good impression! Hmm! Thankfully we were to fly out of Kuching the next day. I went to Sibu and Herb was posted to Simangang. We were already good mates and arranged to meet up again during the school holidays. We did that and on our return back to Britain we remained close friends. Herb was the Best Man at our wedding and he would become an integral part of our family. He came with us when we took our school party to Naples and when the children were born he was their favourite 'Uncle Herbie'. When we moved house Herbie was always there with a large van and at every Christmas he would produce a 'huge' turkey! Everyone loved Herb. He must have been in his 'forties' when he surprised us all by announcing that he was going to get married to a lady recently widowed, who had three children. I remember how both Becca and Sam had worried that he would now be spending his time with his new family, still in Yorkshire, and they might lose him. We reassured them that it would not be so. The wedding was quite elabourate and I was Herb's 'Best Man'. We spent quite a while, before the ceremony, talking through his decision. He had doubts, I know, but I hope no regrets. I think I have only seen Herb twice since that day. He did bring his wife down to Rylands once but we gained the impression that it really 'wasn't her scene' … and many years later he surprised us all when when he turned up at Sam's wedding. Becca had always hoped, throughout her struggle to survive, that he would turn up to see her – but he didn't. And now Bet thought that he would just pop his head round the door.

I finish the chapter of "Why the Whales Came" and Joan asks me if I will send her the book when we have completed reading it. She would like to know how the story ends! Bet's eyes are closed but I know she has been listening and that she has followed the story. How calm she is as Joan strokes her hand. It must be at least two weeks since I have witnessed any anxiety. Herbie featured then.

"I am going home," she firmly told me. "There is a brown car waiting outside. Herbie will drive me. I need my shoes. Put my shoes on!"

"Where are you going?" I asked, just wondering which 'home' she was visualising.

"Fulletby of course. My home. They'll all be there to help me out of the car. They will carry me."

"Shall I come?"

"That's up to you," she said with little enthusiasm. "Just make sure there is enough water for me in the car."

On very rare occasions Bet would smile at me and I would, just for a brief moment, feel that she still loved me. Perhaps now, with Joan and Peter by the side of her bed, she could know that we loved her. I just hope that part of her recognises how I struggled to make her final year as happy as I could.

And everything was a 'struggle' I suppose – although at the time one just has to keep the treadmill turning. Each day it would become a little more difficult to get Bet into the car. Some days we would take the wheelchair but Bet never wanted to be away from her toilet for too long.

"Just drive me round my village. What is it called? I want to live there."

Each day she became more ungainly in the wet room and didn't really want me to invest in a shower stool. Our friendly physiotherapist, another lovely member of our support team, sneaked in with a stool one day. It was there, under the shower the next morning, Bet sat on it, and never a word of complaint. We did the same with a raised toilet seat! I wasn't quite so lucky when I bought in a riser chair. That was never really accepted. She would still prefer me to physically lift her out. Another 'cross' she seemed to want me to bear!

By April I was often using the wheel chair to move Bet around the house – although she could, with help, manage to walk a few paces. The bungalow had been designed for wheel chair use and it certainly worked well. My GP, Dr K, our Admiral Nurse, our CPN, our Speech and Language Specialist – and our miraculous Physiotherapist were frequent visitors. Without their help, and the fact that they would respond to my emails without delay, enabled me to carry on. They all knew that sooner or later I would need extra help. I knew of course! I had known ever since that first diagnosis, but Bet had fought against our every attempt to organise assistance, with anger. As her physical ability was now deteriorating so rapidly we began by reintroducing our friend Mary back into our lives. Mary came along for one morning each week – just to clean the bathrooms and allow me to 'escape' for a couple of hours. Shopping of course – but it still seemed like a lovely break!

It was then agreed that I should have more time for myself and that each morning we would have carers calling to shower Bet. When I say 'agreed', Bet, of course, would never be a willing party to any such arrangement. The first two 'Care Companies' we approached were unable to offer any help. They were fully employed and had no flexibility, particularly in the mornings. We were now face to face with the fact that the care industry is struggling to survive. For a few days it seemed that my hopes would be shattered. I had, for a brief moment, thought about jumping off the treadmill. When once that thought has entered one's head then it is doubly hard to keep up the effort. I suggested a compromise. I would accept help in the afternoons – just to allow me to leave the house for a couple of hours.

The first young lady arrived.

"And how much do you weigh?" Bet demanded, staring hard at the girl, who didn't bat an eyelid. 'M' was a treasure of course. She assured me that they were used to such things and I was to enjoy my walk. On my return 'M' reported that there had been plenty of verbal abuse and that Bet had lashed out and kicked – but I was not to worry. 'M' left and told me that the following day 'C' would be coming. 'C' was the owner of the company. Hmm!

Bet was angry. She 'hated that woman' who had been there. How could I leave her? Why did I need to go for a walk? And I could go for a walk anyway! She didn't need any help. Of course I tried in vain to explain, yet again, how it was good for both of us to 'do our own thing' and that it might be interesting for her to meet new people and tell them about her life. The company had also left me their 'Policy Statement' which explained how they reserved the right to withdraw their services if clients physically abused them in any way.

At 2 pm the next day I was ready for my two hours of 'freedom'. A car pulled up and I watched as 'C' got out and headed towards our house. 'C' was Jamaican and sported an amazing head of dreadlocks! My heart sank. What would Bet make of this? I greeted 'C' and immediately ran out of the house. I tried to imagine how Bet would react. I knew 'my Bet' would love the fact that 'C' came from a different culture – but I couldn't anticipate how this 'new Bet' would react. I needn't have worried. Bet had loved the two hours with 'C'. There had been no swearing and 'C' had received no blows! Out had come Bet's 'Childhood Memory Folder' and lots of photographs. 'C' was one of the few of our growing team of support staff who never incurred Bet's wrath. Again there was never the slightest hint in either the content and tone of 'C's' voice that was delivered in a patronising way. Over the next few weeks I was to meet quite a few young carers and I came to admire them all. Some seemed to get on better with Bet – and others had a tough time. In the first week of my 'escapes' I walked miles. The OS map became well folded as I explored this new 'local' area. I think I over-did things. I went swimming in the sea and pounding the hills. It then dawned on me that it might be better just to enjoy a couple of hours 'relaxation' – although that was a state of mind and body which had completely eluded me for the past two years.

It certainly helped to have a little free time for myself. It was also a great consolation to be able to share my grief, if only for a few minutes, with someone else who was experiencing at least a glimpse into my role. Thankfully all the care team had a degree of humour about them and we could laugh at the day's abuse. As soon as our carer drove away Bet would demand that I take her to the toilet. She would have 'managed' for two hours but I would be expected to lift her, put her into her wheel chair , lift her onto her commode (another gem our super physio had secretly delivered!) and then the reverse journey. All this would then take place at ever more frequent intervals. A hoist had been delivered but, as two people were needed to operate it, it remained in its wrapping! Everything was getting harder and Bet was getting ever more exacting.

The care team were then able to offer me half an hour's help every morning and two of them would come in at 10.30 am to give Bet her shower. This was bliss, especially as Bet seemed, usually, to accept this arrangement. She would even allow them to style her hair and, on rare occasions, tell them that 'it would do!'. It certainly gave me time to sort out Bet's breakfast and even have time to eat something myself. Bet was now eating much less and her evening meal became a rather monotonous helping of shepherd's pie swamped in thick gravy. This was her choice. She continued to enjoy soft fruit, followed by chocolate and a tot of whisky. And bags and bags of 'Fisherman's Friends'! For several months swallowing was getting harder and she was frequently 'spitting out' phlegm. With luck this would be into a tissue but she could also just land it onto the table or onto the carpet. Hey ho! Visitors will understand! Hmm! She had decided that "Fisherman's Friends' would help her. They certainly aided the exodus of spittle. Bet would add another lozenge into her mouth as soon as she had finished one. Within days I had stripped the relevant section in Sainsbury's and even Boots couldn't keep up with my demand. Thankfully the internet could help out and I invested in 50 packs at a time. It could have been worse! Think of the positives!

Getting Bet into bed became a nightmare. She would demand sleeping tablets and was never going to be content with the single one prescribed by our GP. I had to buy boxes of natural herbal 'sleeping aids' from Boots and she would swallow them, with increasing difficulty, at 10 pm. I would aim to watch the News and then begin the process of toilet, undressing and into bed which would take me a further half hour. If I could fall into my bed before 11.30 pm I would be lucky. But that would never be the end! Bet would claim that she couldn't get to sleep and that she needed more sleeping tablets. She would scream to get me out of bed again and often it would be 3 am before she finally settled into a sound sleep. She would have totally exhausted herself. And me! She eventually decided that it was useless going to bed as early as 10.30. She would argue and shout until I agreed to delay taking her to bed for a further half hour. Initially I made the mistake of still giving her sleeping tablets at 10. An hour later she was a 'dead weight' with no use in her legs. She crumpled to the ground. All our neighbours had gone to bed and I was reluctant to call for an ambulance. I did eventually manage to get her into her wheelchair and adjusted my body clock accordingly. We all knew, apart from Bet, that I needed a period of 'respite'.

This time it was to be at 'Trevarna' a care home in St Austell. Initially it would be for two weeks but possibly, if by some miracle she was to 'settle' then it could be for longer. St Austell is an hour's drive away but the attraction was that it was now managed by 'A' – our original CPN who had been responsible for arranging Bet's initial 'assessment' at 'Crossroads'. Bet remembered 'A', fairly fondly it seemed, and agreed that it would be interesting to spend a holiday at Trevarna. She was certainly 'fed up' with me and was looking forward, or so we thought, to spending time with some new faces.

On July 21st I managed to get Bet into the car, loaded her travel bag, television and wheelchair, and began the journey. As we drove away from our house she asked me, for the first time, where Trevarna was. I told her that it was at St Austell. She simply said, "That's a long way." She then remained silent until we reached Truro. As we turned right onto the St Austell road all hell let lose! She began to thump me and tried to drag the steering wheel.

"It's a care home! I am not going into a care home!" she screamed. "You have no right to do this to me! How could you! You cannot do this! I will not go!"

Somehow I managed to drive the remaining dozen or so miles. I am not sure how. Bet fought against me as I lifted her from the car and was angry and rude to "A" who greeted us as friends. This was not going to plan? Why should it? Nothing did! Now it went from bad to worse. "A" told us that the following day she was going on holiday for a week in Italy. Hmm! Then we went along corridors, through many locked doors, to what I believed to be 'the quiet wing'. Dr K had told us that Bet would have a room in 'the quiet wing' and that had been an important part of Bet's deal! Hmm! We entered the room, rather sparsely furnished, and immediately we were surrounded by hideous cries from neighbouring inmates. I saw Bet's body visibly shudder. I cried all the way home.

Everyone told me that, as this was 'my' respite, I should try not to visit Bet. Sam would go every few days but I was to try not to worry and find time to relax! How impossible! My GP called me in and spent far more than our allocated time talking with me. She decided I should be 'checked out' and a barrage of blood tests were taken. That is how I came to be diagnosed as 'diabetic'! I wonder just how many thousands of people are 'diabetic' but just don't know. For me it was just another incidental problem, but one that I knew I could conquer. I really don't mind going to see my doctors! I get cuddles! They are ladies! I should explain. Initially, way back in December 2013, I had telephoned the surgery with a cry for help. I had explained that my wife was behaving very strangely and I was having to get up far too many times each night to empty my bladder. I was asked if I minded seeing Dr W who was in her final few months of training to be a GP. She was so understanding and listened to my emotional tribulation with such a genuine concern and, as I stood up to leave the consulting room, she gave me a hug. That simple action was of such comfort. It was the first of many hugs, from the long list of NHS staff who have supported me through the past two years, but I will never forget how reassuring it was that morning, to leave the surgery feeling that I was no longer alone. When the time came for Dr W to move on to a permanent position she arranged a meeting with Bet and I to 'hand over our care' to her friend Dr H. It was such a thoughtful and supportive thing to do and Dr H took over our care with the same degree of genuine concern and compassion. I still get the cuddles but, as Dr H is rather tiny in comparison, I remain seated! It adds to the fun and relieves any potential tension. Thank you!

I will never forget the look of joy on Bet's face when I arrived to collect her from St Austell. She actually told me that she loved me. She told me again, several times, as we drove home. She seemed so happy. There was no aggression. This period of calm and appreciation lasted for about three hours and then, gradually, the tone changed and I was able to detect a degree of agitation. I dreaded what would happen after tea. I had arranged for our care team to put her into bed and to administer her tablets. I couldn't face the nightly battle of wits that had now become the norm. I thought that I was now unable to physically get her into bed and I gave in to those around me who had told me that I had to accept more help. Unfortunately the latest time the care team could manage was 8pm. For four evenings I witnessed Bet's furious fight to remain upright, dressed, and well clear of her bed. For four nights I suffered hours of continual verbal abuse when the carers had scuttled away in their cars, and for four nights I lifted her in and out of bed and onto her commode at half hourly intervals. This was harder for me. She seemed determined to make me suffer. And so I cancelled the evening help.

Bet was now increasingly aggressive. This was the nature of the illness I am sure, but it was as though she was punishing me for having left her at St Austell. And now, just to compound our agony, Bet had the dreaded 'constipation'! I had always worked hard, through her diet, the doctor's senna tablets and various herbal concoctions which Bet still demanded, to keep the bowels moving. Two weeks in Trevarna and all was lost. Bet's stomach was swollen and she complained of pains in her tummy. The District Nurse became an additional member of my support team and I now had to deal with the post-enema trauma and invest in a large pack of rubber gloves.

There were no more car rides out into the countryside.

"What's the name of that village?"

"I want an enema!"

Tuesday 10th November 2015

I'm going in on the train again today, Shirley has had to go into Truro to ask the optician to straighten Ken's glasses again. He keeps having falls and his glasses seem to suffer just as much as he does. Kenwyn has an alarm mat placed against Ken's chair but by the time a carer reaches him he is usually sprawled out on the floor. At least Bet is no longer in any position to be able to get up and walk. I can't remember when she took her last steps. She certainly never walked again after she returned from Trevarna (St Austell) on 4th August. The next month became a nightmare.

I think, for much of this time, I was frightened. Bet's aggression rarely calmed as she physically and verbally attacked almost everyone. It was at this stage that I realised that I could no longer cope. For my own protection, and sanity, I was the one who now kept a diary. I knew that soon I would have to admit defeat and I suppose I wanted to record just how chaotic, unpredictable and soul-destroying my life had now become.

Only hours after we had returned home from Trevarna she was screaming at me. *"I've gone off you!"* would be just the start. Every day I had to endure her wrath.

"I hate you with every fibre of my body. I hope you have a heart attack!" was spit out with such venom that I felt

sure that she would kill me if she had the physical capacity. If she caught hold of me she would dig her nails into my arm and I would have to fight to free myself. I had to feed her tablets into her mouth with a long spoon for she had now begun to bite my fingers if they came close to her. As it was she would bite hard onto the spoon and I feared for her teeth.

By this time I should have known better but I sometimes answered her. It was never a good idea.

> "*I hope you drown. I never want to see you again!*"
>
> "*Who would look after you?*" I asked.
>
> "*You'd be surprised!*"
>
> "*Where is he? I'll take you to him*". This just infuriated Bet and she began screaming, kicking the air, and swearing.
>
> "*I did a poo all by myself*" she exclaimed, attempting to assert the higher ground. She then pulled out her tongue and continued to swear.
>
> *12th August 2015*

After three enemas over the previous week Bet had, at last, a nuclear fall out. Our District Nurses had responded to her pleas for 'an enema' but they would insert the pessary and then leave me to deal with the aftermath. Bet was also beginning to lose control of her bladder but was refusing to wear anything which might have made life easier for me. The washing machine was now rumbling throughout each day.

Bet was now even rude to me in front of everyone

who called to see us. Maggie came to visit just a few days before Bet's birthday on 19th August. I later wrote down the conversation I had heard.

"It's your birthday next week. What would you like?" asked Maggie.

"A new husband!" Bet uttered with a bitterness which sent a shiver down my spine.

"No. Peter looks after you".

"I hate him!"

11th August 2015

Ann and Kevin had called a couple of days later. Bet was still in bed and as soon as they arrived she dismissed them.

"I want to sleep now!"

She then appeared to be asleep until they left. She then demanded that I got her out of bed. I tried to persuade her to wait until her carers arrived at 2pm but she wouldn't wait. She again refused to wear any incontinence pads and complained about having been given enemas.

"I feel offended. They gave me extra laxative and I don't need it. I did a poo all by myself yesterday! I don't need laxatives!"

13th August 2015

I didn't give up trying. As part of her birthday present I gave her a set of rather beautiful knickers which had press-stud flaps. They were pretty and bore no resemblance to the standard incontinence pants which Bet had rejected outright. I had wrapped them in pretty paper, which was torn off and thrown on the floor. Followed immediately by the pants themselves!

Bet was now sleeping more frequently and this was a welcome development. At times her breathing would become shallow and then go into a hyperventilating frenzy and her arm would shake violently. Our GP called on Friday lunchtime and thought that Bet had developed a chest infection. I think Dr H felt that Bet would fall asleep and simply pass away at some stage over the weekend for she organised a daily visit by the District Nurse Team. As it was the weekend they were not the ones I knew from Falmouth. These were based at Helston. They had obviously been briefed to check out my own personal state for they spent a good half hour over a cup of tea gently asking about our life together.

It would be at this point that I would disappear into my bedroom and return with an otter in my arms. It never failed to delight. Bet's unique puppet design created such realistic animals. She had made spiders, simple hand puppets, ever since we had moved to Scarborough. These then were skilfully adapted, with four finger legs, to sheep, puppies and kittens She continued to make soft toys and one day an empty badger body was lying on a chair in our cottage at Rylands. I remember picking it up and playing with it. At one stage my hand entered the head with my lower arm in its body. We had discovered the seeds of an idea. Bet began to work out her design and the concept was established. A fox soon followed. They proved popular with all who met them. Bet was soon supplying local shops and tourist venues.

We had to find a name! "They are only bits of fluff," I remember saying as we drove over Bodmin Moor.

"That's it!" cried Bet. "Bits O'Fluff!" Our 'company" had been born. By 1990 Bet was exhibiting annually at The Royal Cornwall Show and I was able to work with her on the Saturday. I loved the atmosphere, the fun and the banter. It was as though I was on stage again as we demonstrated our 'pets' and almost everyone stopped at our stall and smiled. Sales were high too and we would sell out by the end of the final day. These were Bet's creations and she quietly glowed with a sense of pride. Initially we regarded the venture as a rather profitable hobby but over the next couple of years I began to wonder if I too could be part of this industry. Teaching was changing. The National Curriculum had become, in my mind, far too restrictive and Standard Attainment Targets were being introduced. In themselves there was nothing wrong with assessing young people's progress but I felt that League Tables would distort my ideal of local schools and eventually challenge the equal value principle. Couple that with the fact that I was having interviews for Headships, with little success. This was possibly because my heart was no longer in what teaching was now becoming. Computers were about to take over the construction of the timetable and our children had left Launceston and were now at University. I decided that I too needed to leave. I had taught for thirty years and totally enjoyed every aspect. I now thought that there was a danger I would begin to lose heart. I didn't want to be a miserable teacher. There were far too many of those! We made the decision to work together. We worked out that we could earn enough money to maintain a reasonable life style. We would invest in a motor home, make toys in the winter, and tour the show grounds in the summer. Colleagues were shocked. Some thought that I was mad and others that I was very brave to give up my salary and the security of my job. It wasn't too great a risk for at that stage we had managed to pay off our mortgage, and, after all, our children, in theory at least, were 'off our hands'.

At the end of term, Christmas 1993, I rode out of the final assembly on a mountain bike which my staff colleagues had kindly bought me. How elated I felt riding furiously along all the corridors. The following day I cut out one thousand badger bodies from two vast rolls of fur fabric. They were piled into 'tens' and filled the attic room. Sam's pool table had now disappeared and the space was taken by an old dining table that was to remain my work surface for the next ten years.

There was something reassuring about all the piles of fur that I created. I suppose I was seeing instant success from my efforts. Teaching has long-term aims and it isn't always easy to feel that one has achieved one's targets. It is probably quite different in today's classrooms for 'targets' seem to flourish and 'assessment' is paramount. I'm not convinced of course, but that's the 'left wing trendy' nature of my style. West Country Television had filmed a news item on my departure. "One of the region's leading teachers quits in protest at the introduction of League Tables." I was flattered – and felt that at least I had moved on with a degree of satisfaction.

Now I was working for Bet. We were together again. We had worked the tables together at The Parade Hotel with great style and success. Now we would make and sell our puppets with the same confidence and satisfaction. It felt good. I soon converted our double garage into two sections 'His' and 'Hers'. We invested in an industrial sewing machine for Bet's side and I moved the old dining table into my half. We built up a stock of fur and developed a smooth operation, carefully timed, for we had no intention of working for nothing. This was to be a successful, viable, commercial concern. We began to plan our adventures and bought our small and practical motor home. Each year we would assess our sales and plan accordingly, adding new show grounds and craft fairs, and dropping anything which had disappointed us. We would attend many County Agricultural Shows and select a variety of other venues. We loved 'camping' in the gardens of beautiful country houses where peacocks strutted around our van and setting up on frosty mornings to become part of Christmas magic; we loved wandering around the vast show grounds when all the crowds had left and, above all, we felt part of a very special group of people.

One of our favourites was The Royal Welsh Show at Builth Wells. A local farmer turned all his land into a massive campsite for a week. We had to pay cash to his wife who sat in a horsebox by the gate and then we had to find some reasonably level spot in the crowded hillside encampment. The view was spectacular. We would awaken to look down on the show ground in the valley below. Hot air balloons would already colour the sky and the sun always shone. That's more than can be said for The Royal Cornwall! There are only the Cornish who would put their county show on high exposed ground, with the Atlantic on one side and Bodmin Moor on the other. No wonder that in the craft world The Royal Cornwall is considered the happiest of all the shows!

The furthest show that we attended was The Lincolnshire. That was where we felt part of the family. One year our official camping pitch was behind The Country Landowner's rather pukka marquee. We were rudely told to move and threatened with being reported to the show's organisers. That year Bet's Uncle Lol was President of the Show. We merely smiled politely and put on our stove to make a pot of tea! Bet had quite a few relatives in the area and they all came to the show and all came to watch us at work. There was much admiration for Bet's designs and we were pleased. She deserved the praise.

One show proved hard each year and that was at Windsor Racecourse just before Christmas. It was profitable and one of Bet's favourite cousins lived quite close. So every year we endured the freezing temperatures, snuggling under our cosy duvet and scraping ice from the inside of our windows. On the final day all would thaw and the field would become a mud bath. Fortunately we could always pack up our stall very quickly and drive off before the exit became impassable and the tractors would be called in. We never became upset or depressed, no matter how difficult a show became. Sometimes, if there was a poor footfall, we would become slightly bored. We thrived on an audience and we loved a crowd!

We would sometimes man our stall at a local show alone. One particular summer's day I found myself behind the stall in the Village Hall at St Issey, near to Padstow. I became aware of a woman carefully watching me and smiling. Christhild, from Germany, was totally captivated by the 'otter'. This was indeed our own favourite puppet for it was very realistic and yet surprisingly simple in design. It quickly became our 'best seller' and our most profitable creation. Little did I know, at this point, that Bet and I were destined to become known as 'otter mutter' and 'otter farter' throughout the Rudolph Steiner Schools in Germany. At St Issey charming Christhild introduced me to her equally warm and friendly sister Roswitha. They spent much time asking me all about "Bits O'Fluff" and I discovered that they were teachers. Roswitha had recently retired and Christhild taught 'eurhythmy' in the Steiner Schools around Wupperthal. They each bought an otter. Such interaction was the part of our work that we both particularly enjoyed and I remember describing the two 'German ladies' to Bet over supper that evening.

A week later we returned from a show to a message on the answer phone:

> *"I am the owner of a guest house in Tintagel. The German ladies who are staying with me would like to visit your shop. Could you let me have details please?"*

Of course we didn't have a shop. We were also very busy, for July and August are the months of summer fairs. I am afraid I didn't even reply. A week later another message:

> *"Hello. I am the owner of a guesthouse in Tintagel. I left a message for you last week but you obviously didn't receive it. I will try again. I have some German guests who are very keen to get in touch with you. Where can they find you? Please get in touch!"*

This time I did respond and apologised. I explained that we didn't have a retail outlet other than at shows. I gave a list of shows during the following couple of weeks where we were scheduled to be making an appearance but they were not close to Tintagel and therefore I didn't expect to see or hear from the German ladies again. One Thursday, at 8 am, we had just constructed our showcase in a rather ragged tent at Okehampton Show when we became aware of a small group of people watching us. I recognised

Roswitha and Christhild but they had a further three people with them. We were introduced to Margaret, a matriarchal figure who we later discovered had been a leading dance practitioner in the Steiner world, to Karin, a retired teacher of English, and to Aivars, a twenty-year-old Latvian young man who was a student of dance. They were totally besotted by our collection of puppets. They worked their way through our entire stock with delight and much animated laughter. They all bought at least one puppet. It was a lovely start to our day. We knew they were about to return home and we were flattered that they had made the long journey to find us, and at such an early time! We had no idea of the impact we had made on them!

A few weeks later we received a letter from Germany. It was from Roswitha asking if we could send her eight otter puppets. We were into International Marketing! I wasn't quite sure how to deal with the financial side but it certainly excited the local post office when I turned up with the carefully addressed package. That was just the start. By Christmas we had 'exported' over one hundred puppets. They were being sold at the Steiner Christmas Markets and were apparently proving so very popular. The following summer Roswitha and Christhild returned to North Cornwall. This time they arrived with a list of various 'animals' and collected them before returning to Germany. They sent us a lovely photograph taken on the ferry. The car was packed full of puppets but they had the windows open so that they could breath! That summer we met up with them several times and they came over to 'Rylands' to have lunch with us and also helped us harvest our magnificent crop of blackcurrants. They became our friends.

And so over the years we had a couple of visits to Germany. We were taken to visit many Steiner Schools and both of us were impressed by what we saw and heard. Whenever we arrived we were introduced as 'otter mutter' and 'otter farter' and it seemed that everyone knew of our puppets. We were famous! Aivars, the young man from Latvia, came over to Cornwall to work for us in order to improve his English. His German girl friend arrived a few days later, which rather surprised us as she already had excellent English. We had offered to help one person – but not two! It didn't faze Bet however. She calmly made them both a welcome part of our family, and set them interesting and suitably challenging tasks in the workroom. At the same time she encouraged them in developing their language skills and, as we all worked and played together, she would correct any grammatical points and aid their pronunciation. We would take breaks from sewing and go for walks on Bodmin Moor where Aivars would relish the freshness of the air and respond through his movements to the sharpness of the wind. He was mentally working through his thesis in which he was aiming to explore the relationship between the wilds of the North Cornish Coastal scenery and the importance of eurhythmic dance movements in the Steiner system of education. Bet and I both found this fascinating. Interesting that, today, the value of linking physical activity with learning is becoming more valued in our schools. Of course, as a teacher of Drama, I had always seen a valid relationship.

Time was not on Aivars' side. He had been given a month to write his long-overdue thesis. Without this he would be unable to graduate and he needed to qualify as a teacher within the Steiner system. I decided to try to help him. He would talk through his ideas with me. His English was not very well developed but he had an incredible ability to understand me – and to make me understand him. He seemed unable to write down his ideas. There was a block somewhere. It wasn't his German, for he could speak and write fairly fluently. It was when we talked about his education in Latvia that I realised his problem. The schools had been heavily controlled by Russia. His written work had been expected to be largely factual. He needed now to free his mind and to realise that he could write poetically and with imagination. As he wrote sections in long hand, I offered to type his work. I had no idea what an ordeal I had embarked on. Typing up a thesis in German, a language I know nothing of, was not easy! Miriam would correct any grammatical errors and then we printed out the completed work and placed it in a smart presentation folder. We have a photograph of Aivars handing the folder to his tutor at 10 pm on the evening when midnight was the deadline! Aivars and Miriam later married and had two sons. As far as I know, they are both still teaching in Germany. Sadly Roswitha and Christhild both died of cancer within a few months of each other. Margaret too has passed away but Karin is still alive and in a nursing home in Schloss Hamborn. They all became such a lovely part of our family – thanks to the 'otter'!

We made thousands of otter puppets. Wherever we appeared the 'otter' caught the attention of everyone who passed by. Every year at Tiverton Show young children would call out with glee "There's Ottie!" We asked who 'Ottie" was and it was explained that he belonged to a teacher, Mrs Williams, at one of the local primary schools. She had one of our puppets in her classroom and would allow a child, one who had been the most socially positive during the day, to take 'Ottie' home for the evening. This was on the condition that the child read 'Ottie" a story. Obviously her technique worked, judging by the thrilled smiles we witnessed every year. I would pass on this story to any teacher who bought a puppet from us. A few years later we were able to meet Mrs Williams when she came to buy another otter puppet as her poor 'Ottie' was getting rather worn! We were able to tell her that she had had far more influence on encouraging the nation's children to read than the whole of the government's Literacy strategy!

Sam spent a year teaching in London whilst Ian was managing Kensington's David Lloyd Leisure Gym. She had a fox cub puppet called 'Spike' whose 'mum and dad' were still in the workshop in Cornwall. The children in Sam's class at Flora Gardens wrote copious letters to Spike's family – and Bet and I had great fun replying! In fact we got quite a few lovely letters from satisfied customers – especially at Christmas time when our mail orders really flooded in. It was a great time and we both had fun. I am sure Bet loved this period.

Whenever we set up at a show we would meet up with 'old friends' – and come to know 'new' craftspeople. It was a kaleidoscope of skilled, interesting people – shaken up at the end of every show and spilled out in different combinations in fields, country houses and village halls throughout the country. It is a very special world of very talented and artistic people who display very special skills. Many had held professional roles in the 'proper world' and had rejected the security of a salary for a far more satisfying, if unpredictable, life of creativity. They would never get rich but they would enjoy their life. That is what we did – although I could never claim to have any real skill. I watched with awe. I remember one particular craft show held in a public school. The Head, with his gown flowing behind him, made a very condescending flounce round the stalls as a gesture of thanks. After he left, I calculated that there were probably more graduates behind the stalls than he had in his staff room. How do we judge people?

As for the idea of schools – I often reflected on how much my students could have learned, of skills and life, by spending a few hours with each of these talented individuals. We met a few families who were 'self educating'. They were 'onto a winner' as my Dad would have said! I think we both gained a tremendous insight into many art forms. Bet, particularly, soaked up information about flowers and herbs and, especially, their healing qualities. She continued to give her time to help anyone who asked for help with their physical well-being. She was always careful to explain that she could offer no cures but the people who came to visit were people who had explored all the options that conventional medicine had to offer. So many people left the tranquillity of 'Rylands', and Bet's capacity to listen, with hope. Whether her crystals or her interest and brief training into kinesiology and reflexology had anything to do with this – I will never know. She helped, in her quiet and unassuming way, a great number of people.

Our puppets too were found to be of value in a wide variety of therapy. We heard many heart-warming accounts of how our 'pets' had brought comfort and companionship, to elderly people in care homes and hospitals; they were found to be invaluable to some psychiatric teams, especially where young children were being encouraged to communicate their feelings; we had reports from doctors and dentists who used them in their surgeries; and, of course, they found their way into a great number of classrooms. Bet gained so much satisfaction from all the positive feedback. Of course, making hundreds of puppets was a monotonous activity but we added new designs each year and Bet would always respond to individual requests. There was the vicar who wanted a large sheep for his Christmas sermon. That was fun and the life-size creation became part of our stock. The next year he requested a dove. This wasn't quite as angelic as Bet would have liked but it did result in quite a naughty seagull being created. The next year the vicar asked for a camel. Bet produced one but was far from happy! That was the last request from that particular church!

I often quote a particularly cold and wet Friday evening when we were setting up in a marquee at Broadlands, just a few miles north of Southampton. The marquee was bitterly cold as the organisers were having trouble with their generators. That meant we had limited lighting. It did not bode well. Setting up next to us was an elderly lady who had 'woolly hats'! I remember raising my eyebrows and wondering how on earth we were going to get any fun from this weekend. I needn't have worried. This lovely lady had worked for Group Captain Cheshire and had opened and run his care home in the Himalayas. What captivating and informative stories she told us over the next two days. She now sold her knitted hats in order to fund an annual holiday for herself and her husband at The Island Hotel on Tresco. I do hope that they had a lovely holiday the next summer – and for a good few more years. Behind every stall was an interesting story!

Recently I have just occasionally wondered if Bet really did enjoy "Bits O'Fluff" as much as I thought she did. Over the past months, whenever I have brought out an 'otter' to show people she has emphasised that the puppets were all her own designs and then added that it was very hard work. No matter how strange or unexpected Bet's comments are, I am never able to completely dismiss them. She does not exist in a totally 'different world' and I can never ignore the implications of what she says. Perhaps we did work too hard? Perhaps we should have taken time out and had more 'adventures'? But we did! Life was a complete adventure and I am sure that she appreciated this! I know, at one stage, we created a full time job for Steve, Becca's partner at that time. With two units 'on the road' we had to double our output. That was certainly additional pressure but typically Bet willingly took on the challenge in order to help out a friend.

Working with Bet for ten years on the craft scene was never short of fun and excitement. Every show was unique. We would meet up with friends old and new and thousands of people would smile! We would judge our success, not necessarily on sales, but on the laughter we had created. Just as when we had first been paired together in the hotel restaurant in Skegness all those years ago, the happiness of our customers was paramount. The fact that our care often resulted in 'good tips' was a reward for which we felt grateful. Just as, whenever we drove away from a show ground, Bet would open our money belts and do a swift count. We did have fun! I am convinced of that.

Only when my Mum reached a point, at 91 years old, where she needed help with everyday living, did we call our itinerant adventures to a halt. In our final year we had cancelled our long trips away and we concentrated on 'day shows' which were in reasonable driving distance. We no longer camped and part of the joy was lost. It now really did become hard work. My sister Pauline had made her own decision to move into residential care at nearby Bowden Derra. She was happy there and we were grateful for that. Bet's parents were no longer with us and Becca, now teaching, had borrowed money from us to buy her own house in Launceston. Bet and I would turn the page once more and begin a new life. This time we would be mum's carers and we would live in Bodmin just to please her.

I look at poor Bet now. She lies unable to move her frail body. Just a few years ago she had so much energy and was full of life. I think of her sewing away for hours at a time. I remember the speed with which she would set up our colourful stall. I remember how we would walk in the evenings through the woods at The Royal Show in Warwickshire with, as it had been a very dry summer, real badgers by our feet as they scavenged through the leaves for food. I remember the nightingale's song at Littlecote House; the gigantic Greek supper after a show in Brighton Pavilion; walks by the Thames with the trees above crowded by what we assumed were parakeets, and glasses of wine on a field with the sun setting beyond the trees. I try to share these memories with Bet as she lies before me. I can never say all that I want to say. I must find a way. For I know that time is now limited.

I also know that her body is failing. She has constipation and her stomach is distended. Today, however, there is no mention of an enema.

"Your balls in a Sandwich!"

Thursday 12th November 2015

It is 10.30 am and Sam and I are hurrying along the corridor towards Bet's room. We have no idea whether Bet is still alive. At 9 am this morning I had realised that there were two urgent messages on my answer phone. I had slept through them both. The Sister in charge of Bet's section at Kenwyn was concerned about Bet's state and was anxious that I should come in as soon as I could. I called Sam and she was immediately 'released' from her classroom and came round to collect me.

As we drove into Truro I was able to talk through what we were likely to find. I was not surprised to hear that Bet was probably near to death. The day before she had been in a very strange state. Her breathing had been very heavy and laboured, there were rasping and gurgling sounds deep in her lungs, and her skin grey. At times it was as though she was delirious and I told Sam the last words she had spoken. I could just distinguish them for her speech was now failing.

"*I want your balls in a sandwich!*" she had croaked. Search as I might, but I could find no sign that this was said in jest – or as the result of some distant memory of loving times.

"That sums it up doesn't it! Your Mum's last words to me!" I said to Sam, trying hard not to betray just how hurt I had felt.

That would fit so well with her last diary entry:

"I went three times today"
Bet Kaye 10th July 2015

An absolutely beautiful life. Why does it all have to end like this?

Bet's door is wide open which is a good sign. We peep round the corner. Bet is lying in her bed, awake and looking around at us. She has had a shower and looks far better than she had done the day before. Sister L is apologetic and explains how Bet's breathing had been so laboured when the day staff had come on duty. The doctor will see her again later in the day. I have already spoken to the GP team and been assured that a syringe-driver will readily be fitted if Bet appeared to be in pain or suffering in any way. I felt reassured. I had been through this routine before as I watched my elder daughter leave her life behind. I knew the score.

I know death will come soon to Bet. I have those mixed confused feelings, and in one sense I am now feeling a degree of disappointment. The sooner all this suffering is over then, perhaps, life can be reclaimed. I know this seems selfish – and totally irrational. Life will never be the same. And what will I do when I don't have Bet any more? I feel very guilty for I have plans.

Sam and Ian have offered to convert part of their home into a 'granddad cave' and I have already placed the bungalow on the market to release the necessary funds. I know it is important to have future plans and I am aware that there is a vast void looming into which I could easily fall. But it still feels totally wrong. Just as it does when my mind goes to thinking about Bet's funeral. I've already warned Paula, my lovely undertaker! She understands that we will arrange something personal and suitably fitting to celebrate Bet's life. At this time, however, I cannot see further than Bet's poor body lying before us.

Sam and I take over from the staff and the routine begins. Bet manages to savour a little yoghurt, and some rhubarb and strawberry puree which I placed in the fridge yesterday when she refused all help. We clean her teeth, moisten her lips with her balm, and rub her legs and arms with her 'Hippy Rose'.

Sam has been a tremendous support. I know the personal dilemma that she has faced over the past year as she has tried to balance her desire to teach with the fact that she knows I have been struggling to look after her mum. I know how much she wanted to have a permanent teaching post instead of the maternity covers she had recently been offered, She wanted her 'own classroom' and her 'own class of children' with the stability that they offer. I remember the mixed feelings I had when she applied for her present full-time post. I was tired and it would have been so comforting to have her by my side. I knew that when once term began she would be fully committed to her classroom and her children. Sam is very conscientious and although her school was sympathetic to her home situation I knew that I would have to cope on my own for most of the time. As it turned out, we moved Bet into Kenwyn very shortly after term began. Sam didn't have to tear herself apart. I hope she doesn't feel any guilt. Life has to go on and she is a mum and a wife herself.

Sam had recognised for a long time that eventually I would have to relinquish my care of Bet. It was just so hard for me to accept that I was no longer able to cope. The needs that Bet had were complex and it was now really impossible for one person to manage. As I now read back through my own notes I realise how unpredictable and challenging life had become. I was getting very little sleep and even after living in this uncertain state for two years I was still finding myself getting irrationally distressed by the things Bet verbally hurled at me.

"My mother always said I should have married Herb! She said you were a homosexual!" Bet spit out at me one evening shortly after I had brought her home from St Austell.

I should never have become upset but it still plays on my mind. Her mum would never have said such a thing – or would she? Where were the seeds for this statement? I knew that occasionally Bet's seemingly random comments did have a tiny degree of logic and could be traced to something in her past. I know I taught drama and have never liked football. Hmmm! Even worse I once wore a purple suit that Bet had made for me! Deeper searching was triggered as I sat looking over at her angry face staring wildly at me. As a young teenager I had been involved in a touch of 'gay play' but that was because my mother had terrified me with her abhorrence of unwanted pregnancy and my resultant fear of touching any hidden part of a girl's anatomy. I had even been 'abused' I suppose – although I quite enjoyed the sensation when C (a family friend) put his hand into my shorts. I suppose I wasn't too sure, at that stage of my life, where my sexuality was leading. But by the time I was in the Sixth Form, and certainly at College, I had no doubts. No Bet! If your mum did say I was a 'homosexual' she was wrong. I wanted to remind Bet of the prolific and fulfilling physical side of our relationship that we had so much enjoyed but I know this would have upset her. I know that for the past year she has felt physically abandoned. My 'libido' had been drained by my treatment and by the other stresses in my life. Sadly, I was also afraid to become too close for fear of being physically attacked. I did keep trying to cuddle her, not easy whilst trying to avoid thumps and kicks, but was always rejected. She would continue to attempt masturbation, although now virtually impossible and more of a defiant act, at frequent intervals and accuse me of neglecting her needs.

A record over a typical 24 hours :

Peter Kaye 28th August 2015

2.30   Bet eventually settled. I attempted to get some sleep. I awoke after an hour as I needed a wee. Bet asleep

06.00   Bet called me. She wanted to sit on the commode. It was a struggle. She hit me several times. I managed a little more sleep.

9.15	Bet shouted and screamed. She wanted a cup of tea. Another lift on and off the commode. She no longer has any strength in her legs. The hospital bed helps. I got up, showered and prepared breakfast. Bet slept which was good.
10.30	Wanted commode. No bowel movement. Wanted breakfast in bed. Helped her.
10.50	District Nurse. Bet demanded an 'enema' and Nurse obliged and left
11.30	Commode. Bowel movement. Soiled sheet so changed. Bet back to bed
12.10	Commode. Bowel movement. Back to bed. TV on. Relatively quiet period so washer on and prepared some lunch
12.45	Bet wanted to get up. Commode. Dressing. Into wheelchair. To kitchen for lunch. Small sandwich. Some mashed peach and grapes. Tiny portion. Needed help.
13.10	Move to lounge. Transfer from wheelchair to chair. Wanted TV on. Yawning loudly Repeating "I am tired" Asks for 'epitizer' (epilator) corrected to 'escalator'.
14.15	Carers arrive and give Bet a shower. Afterwards she wanted to return to bed. I had a walk
16.15	I have been away. Carers leave. Immediately demands commode. Back to bed. Asks for a lemon sandwich? Those things that grow in the garden (lettuce) Make her a very small one.

16,50	Wanted to get out of bed. Commode, Dressed again. Insists on pants (so hard to get on and off) Sheet soiled again. Wheelchair to lounge. Transfer to chair. TV.
17,50	Wanted tea. Prepared very small shepherds pie with thick gravy. Wheelchair to table. Ate very little. Small helping of strawberries and cream. Talks about 'Sue and Ian' but is confused as she means 'Sam and Ian'. Verbally aggressive.
18,50	Back to chair. Then asks for commode. Lift her again. Pants down. Getting a struggle. I can't go on doing this. Watches TV. Says she is afraid of me and that she has bad thoughts. Says she hates me and hopes I die soon. I give her a whisky and some chocolate. She kicks me.
20,00	Wants to go to bed as she hates me (very unusual at this early time). Wants her sleeping tablets etc. Am getting tablets mixed up. I have difficulty in concentrating.
20,15	Commode. Undressed. Teeth etc. Thumping me. Still verbally abusive. TV in bedroom. She then calls me every few minutes. She wants her glasses. She wants a 'Fisherman's Friend'… more sleepers… the commode… to tell me that she loathes me and wants Sam to look after her… she wants to spit… the commode again. Asking for Herb. Asking to go to the Duchy. Needs another enema. Repeating "I am afraid of you"
00,00	I eventually get to bed

02,00	Awoken by shouting. More sleeping pills as she claims she hasn't been to sleep. I used to argue but now give her two more natural tablets via Boots! Commode. She hits me and tries to kick. Getting her back into bed is hard. It must hurt her. She begins to scream – very loudly – and I cover her head with a pillow. Just briefly but the thoughts are there! Would this be the kindest thing to do?
03,00	Up again
05,00	Again. Help me! Please.

Of course I hated myself for having lost control but, sadly, it was happening far too frequently. A few nights previously Bet had violently lashed out at me as I tried to lift her from commode to bed. I smacked her back, quite hard across her arm. She began to scream. A very loud artificial scream rather like a toddler in a paddy! I pleaded with her to stop – eventually shouting that I thought she was a 'selfish cow!' Heaven knows where I dragged that choice phrase from but it was effective. She stopped screaming. She then began to cry but there were no tears.

"I have cried all my tears away," she said quietly. *"I have none left."*

I went to my bedroom. I had tears for both of us.

The care team were suffering Bet's frustrations too. One morning she became particularly angry as they had found it impossible to take her into the wet room. She demanded that they washed her hair but they didn't have the right equipment. "Bugger off!" Bet screamed at them. The poor girls were due back on duty that same afternoon. At lunch time our GP popped by.

"Wash my hair!" Bet screamed at her.

"I'm sorry I can't do that," said Dr H forgetting for a moment, and getting too close. Whack!

"Bugger off then!"

I had to smile. It was quite funny but I hope our dear Dr H wasn't too badly bruised. That afternoon the care team returned and prepared some strawberries for Bet. The following day they managed to wash her hair. Lovely girls they are and totally undervalued by society.

It became even harder for she was now really losing control of her bladder and still fighting against wearing anything resembling incontinence pads. I bought pads for the bed but there were now 'accidents' over the floor. I spent all my time, it seemed, lifting her and dodging her thumps or filling and emptying the washing machine. I emailed the 'support team' and told them that I could no longer cope. There was no advice about where best to place Bet. There was no really 'suitable' nursing home that anyone knew of. Again it would be up to me.I would have to make the decision – tired and stressed that I was.

Whenever I had a few minutes I would try to research on the internet. I sent for brochures and telephoned homes to find out if suitable beds might be available. It was the usual story. Sam came with me over the Bank Holiday weekend as we viewed a selection of nursing homes which claimed to have some experience of motor neurone disease. We were appalled by one where we had had to climb over patients slumped in wheelchairs in the dark dismal corridors. Another seemed bright and very caring but unfortunately only had a bed in a double room. That just would not have worked. Only Kenwyn really impressed us. It was clean and the newly refurbished area was more in the style of a luxury hotel. The nurse who took us around was genuine and compassionate. We saw patients involved in various activities and there was plenty of space in the dining room and lounges. There was a large garden too. Bet would appreciate that. Of course the fees were high and I was told that I would need to 'top up' by £400 each week. I was now prepared for this however and knew that as Bet was entitled to 'Continuing Health Funding' then the NHS should cover the whole cost. Asking for 'top up fees' seems to have become the norm although my interpretation of the rules is that this is illegal.

I told Kenwyn that I wanted Bet in there as soon as possible and I wrote to the funding group to ask them to fully fund this final stage in Bet's life. They agreed, although there were several days of bureaucratic delays which I found very stressful A date was set. I would take Bet into Truro on the morning of Thursday 10th September. The care team would come in at 10.30 as usual, wash and dress Bet, and then help me to lift her into my car. That would work well.

Our GP, however, was concerned that Bet might physically fight me as she had done on our last journey into care. She arranged for an ambulance to collect us by 11am. That would be good. I tried to prepare Bet and told her about Kenwyn. I assured her that it was a beautiful hospital and not a care home. I lied again when I told her that it was part of the Duchy Hospital and that it shared the same team of nurses. I told her about the beautiful gardens and the fact that it was surrounded by trees. She quietly seemed to accept that it would be a good place to go. I thought all would be well. Did anything ever go to plan?

By 11am on the Thursday morning Bet was washed and neatly dressed and ready for the arrival of the ambulance. The carers had to move on and we waved to them as they drove away. No ambulance arrived and Bet was becoming agitated. By 11.30 she wanted the commode so I had to manouvre her out of the wheelchair. There were no short cuts. She was fully dressed. I wanted to leave her on the commode until the ambulance arrived and I would have some help but Bet did not want that. I eventually man-handled her back into her pants and her chair! By 12.30 pm there was still no sign of an ambulance and we had just survived our third journey onto the commode. Bet was now really angry – and hungry! I telephoned the surgery and eventually they traced the 'error in the system' and I was assured that an ambulance was now on its way. I asked from where it was coming but the surgery had forgotten to check that part of the story. Cornwall is a large county! It eventually arrived at 2pm – three hours late and both Bet and myself were in quite distressed states.

The ambulance team were female – which,as far as Bet was concerned, was a distinct disadvantage. They were of course caring and efficient and it wasn't their fault that we had been waiting for three hours. Immediately they entered the room Bet attempted to take charge.

"I am not going to a nursing home!" she stormed. "Take me to the Duchy!"

She continued to repeat this throughout the careful pushing, pulling and strapping of herself and her chair into the ambulance. The ambulance team reassured her that she would be taken to The Duchy and she seemed to settle. I decided to follow in my car.

The ambulance drove off and I realised that the decision had now been made. Bet would, from this point onwards be in the care of others. My fight was over. There could be no turning back. I emptied the commode and looked round at all the hoists and equipment which filled our bedroom. It was all dead now. Finished with! All that effort and potential support and still I felt as though I had failed. This was not how it should be. It wasn't the first time, of course, that Bet had gone into care but this was different. I knew it was final. I knew now as I stood in the silent house that my Bet would never return. I just hoped that Kenwyn would be kind to her.

They were and for the first few days Bet appreciated the afternoon 'activities'. On the second day we were entertained by a selection of owls, beautifully patient and tame birds, brought in from the county's sanctuary. The following afternoon there was a singer who completed a two hour session, with his keyboard, belting out classic oldies. Those were the only two sessions which Bet attended. She seemed to have lost interest and her body was tired. Only once did she ask to come home, just for a night, and she seemed to accept that this pleasant room with its view out onto the garden was a comfortable place to rest. This made it so much easier for me.

That was nine weeks ago. Each day Bet has become weaker. Her body can no longer support itself; her eye sight has almost failed; she can no longer eat and can barely drink; and now her voice is slurred and distorted. Before Sam and I set off home I ask her if she still would like me to bring her a sandwich. She becomes more alert and grunts approval.

"Will you manage with a strawberry jam sandwich?" I ask her with a grin.

She nods and I detect what would have been a radiant smile. My Bet is still there!

I will bring her a jam sandwich tomorrow. Tonight there will be no need to stew my testicles!

"My Friend Walter"

Tuesday 17th November 2015

I arrive with a bunch of flowers. Bet loves flowers and I have always made sure there are colourful displays in her room. This time I've gone for the brightest blooms, for I know that Bet's sight is now failing rapidly. The alstroemerias which Hazel and Richard had brought in a few days earlier are still glowing and Bet opens her eyes and I know that she can appreciate the beauty. She had enjoyed seeing Hazel and Richard too – for she rarely failed to recognise our friends. Richard and his mum had owned the 'village shop' in Altarnun. I know Richard and Hazel's hearts would have been in tears when they saw Bet lying helplessly in her bed, for they would remember that energetic Bet who had carried down strawberries, blackcurrants and potatoes to 'sell' on the stall outside the shop – the harvest of her Ryland's joy. Towards the end of our time at Rylands Bet and I had looked after the shop on occasions and this enabled Richard and Hazel to have short holidays. 'Richard's Shop' was the centre of village life and the focus of all the local gossip. There was plenty of material here for another book should I ever complete this one! Our dear friend Jain, also from Altarnun, had met me in Truro yesterday and she too had sat with me here by the side of Bet. Jain is a very special friend for we share such tragic pathways.

One of Jain's lovely children took her own life whilst she was in the Sixth Form; her husband Paul was diagnosed with metastatic melanoma at the same time as Becca's collapse; and Jain herself had since fought her way through treatment for breast cancer. Now she is sharing all this with me. I do so appreciate this, for I know the memories which must flood her mind and I understand, as much as anyone else can, the trauma she has survived. I think we both know the meaning of a 'broken heart'.

I tell Bet that Fran and Jennie will come again on Saturday. She utters approval. I know she responds well to Fran – especially his ability to play the intelligent fool. On their last visit he had spent much of the time singing and Bet had joined in remembering all the lyrics. I am not sure whether she will sing this time. I'm not good at singing. I remember Becca asking me to sing "Puff the Magic Dragon" just a few days before she died. I never finished the song – and she knew why.

I offer Bet a little yoghurt and then clean her mouth and her teeth. Her lips are cracked and her tongue is dry. She finds it hard to swallow the water I offer. What I need, I realise, are some moist swabs. I ask the staff but it seems they do not have any and they would need to be prescribed. When I get home I will order some on Amazon!

Katie has selected yet another book from her Michael Morpurgo collection – "My Friend Walter". Bet's eyes are closed but I know she hears and understands. Walter was her dad's name and I know that she loved him so dearly.

I begin to read and get as far as the second paragraph.

"Around me at home there's my family. First there's Father, who's a farmer. Father treats me like a boy. I think he always wanted me to be a boy really. Then there's Mother, who's always busy. If she's not out on the farm she's scurrying about the house with a broom or a pile of dirty washing..."

I am unable to continue reading. My eyes have filled with tears and my voice is choking. I have to sort this out. Even reading is now becoming hard for me to do. This is pathetic. I grab myself a glass of water and try to talk to Bet again. There is so much I want to share.

What do I select from a lifetime of adventure? What images? What do I want to achieve as I sit by Bet's bedside? I want Bet to reverberate again with laughter. I want to know that she has enjoyed being part of our lives. I suppose I need to reassure myself that our journey, our life together, has been a partnership – and not just a self-indulgent trip.

"Do you remember when we visited Fran and Jennie in Madrid?"

Bet does. I know she remembers well. I want to continue. I want to voice all those images of driving across France and Spain on the last family holiday we all experienced together. I want us to share again the rustic charm of Brittany and the canoe trip down the Dordogne. I want us to both laugh about leading Becca and Sam, as reluctant teenagers, up to the beautiful Pyrenean col Bet and I had discovered as mere teenagers ourselves way back in the early sixties. It had been a long haul and we had reassured them as we climbed above the tree line, that the view would be worth every hard step. As we reached the top and that long promised vista we heard the sound of cars. Before us was a car park and the sight of tourist buses. The girls were not impressed. So much for progress. It was a long slog back to the campsite where Sam and Becca healed their grievance by watching the Andorran football team in practice.

I decide not to voice all the memories I so much want to share again. I sense that Bet feels sad for that life, that vitality and energy which are now beyond her reach. I feel that she now has no alternative but to accept that her body has moved beyond repair. She may still hold me responsible; she may still feel that I failed to find the right chiropractor or place her into that healing, magical place – The Duchy; she may still hate me for placing her here – away from home. I will never know again what she is thinking. That is so hard. Wherever we have travelled it has been a totally shared experience. Hasn't it? The nods and asides, the under-breath comments, the knowing smiles – all those warm, comforting gestures of shared companionship – I want to know them again. Please don't leave me alone.

"Do you remember when we visited Fran and Jennie in Singapore?"

That had been our first call on what we affectionately called our 'World Trip' of 1992. The girls were both at

University and we decided to head for New Zealand and visit my Uncle Tom. Now there was a character!

My first memories of my Uncle Tom were when I was about three years old. He was young, handsome and in uniform. He had been in the army, seeing this as an easier life than slaving down the mine with his father and brother. Now he was in the Dock Yard Police in Hong Kong and my mind was captivated by the stories he told. One evening he arrived at our house with a parrot in a cage – and I think it was a gift for me. Sadly my mother quickly made him take it back to The Three Horse Shoes but the image stayed with me. My Uncle Tom was a romantic adventurer who travelled the world. He became my hero!

A few years later my grandmother (that's Granny Kettles) received a letter from her youngest son. Tom had written to say that he was going to get married to Esme and that he was returning with her to her native New Zealand. The letter gave no forwarding address and Granny was asked not to try to make contact. Tom promised to write later and explain. That promised letter never came and I think it broke Granny Kettle's heart. Granddad had little sympathy for he had little faith in his itinerant son. He believed that Tom had got himself into trouble and would now be in gaol. Granny would have nothing to do with this theory and Tom's photograph was moved to the centre of the sideboard replacing those of my father and his sister Estella. I often tried to talk to Granny about Tom but the subject would soon be changed. She died not knowing what had become of her son.

It must have been almost forty years later when Tom suddenly reappeared into my life. My Mum and Dad, after their retirement, had invested in a holiday caravan at Ulrome on the East Yorkshire coast. One sunny afternoon as my dad sat in his deck chair wearing his flat cap, the owner of the caravan park came rushing towards him.

"Hey up Bert! 'As tha' gorra brother in New Zealand?"

"I had one but heaven knows if I still have!" My father was stunned.

"He's on't phone for thee!"

My father spoke to his young brother again. It was, by all accounts, a very emotional experience on both sides of the planet. Tom was to ring me a few hours later. I was elated. I was to talk to my hero, my world traveller, and my explorer! The moment we spoke I must admit to a hint of disappointment. I had quickly to readjust my image. Tom still had a very thick Barnsley accent, itself accentuated by long distance telecommunications. This wasn't quite the 'James Bond image' that the missing years had cultivated.

Tom was to visit us all in Cornwall a year later. Sadly my father had died just before we left Scarborough. That would have been such a lovely reunion to be able to witness. By now we knew the full story. Tom had married Esme, a girl from New Zealand and had gone AWOL! In order to protect his parents he had not given them any details. He fully intended to write – but he never did. The longer he left writing – the harder it became. He then became afraid of bad news and it was only after Esme had died that his friends had persuaded him to try to make contact again with his family. He had telephoned 'The Three Horse Shoes' and asked for news of my father. Amazingly the link was formed that led to the caravan park.

And so Tom, and his lovely new partner Lorna, came into our lives at Rylands. And now, a further ten years down life's line, Bet and I were heading out on a return visit to Pakuranga in the outer suburbs of Auckland. By now I had accepted the warmth of the Barnsley accent (which, by the way, is the one I still cling to when I need the comfort of my roots) and the extended tummy – and, I suppose, even the flat cap! En route we planned a variety of experiences. Singapore had changed beyond recognition. Fran, Jennie and their children Robin and Rachel lived in a 'condominium' – so to experience the city we had to board the condominium bus, pass by the condominium guards and through the condominium gates! My upward gaze could scarcely find the sky – scraped indeed by the concrete of progress. And where was the sea now? Bet was in her element. I remember her delight at the incense-filled temples, the fruit and vegetable stalls, the gardens, the hawkers frying the nasi goreng, the whole cacophony of sounds and smells which attacks the senses. This was the Far East that I had always wanted to share with Bet.

Our next flight took us over the South China Sea and then, below us, the jungle of Sarawak. This had been my home for a year and a half in 1965/66 and

I wanted Bet to experience as much of this beautiful country and its lovely people as we could cram into one week. Of course materially it had changed dramatically and in some ways I resented the new roads, the high-rise buildings and the glossy shopping centres but thankfully they had catered fairly sensitively for tourists. The Hilton, in Kuching, greeted us with a basket of tropical fruits; the cultural village seemed staffed by native groups who were happy to show their lost heritage; the museum provided the necessary history – and the people were full of smiles. On our move to Sibu we were, thankfully, even closer to the local folk. We stayed in the home of a Chinese family. We had met Fidelia a year earlier. She was a teacher who had come over to Britain to further her studies at Plymouth. We met her at a party in North Cornwall and discovered that her home was in Sibu – the town where I had taught on my VSO posting. There was no hesitation in inviting her to share a Christmas at Rylands – and now, typical of Chinese generosity, she wanted to repay our kindness. Her elderly parents gave up their bed for us and Fidelia and her sister drove us around. Bet was able to sit cross-legged on the veranda of an Iban long house; to watch marjong being played in a Chinese coffee shop; to be a guest at a Malay wedding; to see Chung Hua where I taught and to meet some of my fellow teachers; to see pepper being harvested; to taste the full spiced flavours of local cooking and to make friends with everyone we met.

I am now holding Bet's hand as she lies, eyes closed, listening to my ramblings. I am slowly listing the places we visited and just hoping that the memories are good for her. She will remember. Her memory has always been sharper than mine. I move us onto Melbourne. She will remember arriving at 5am and being met by Lay Eng and Terry. Lay Eng was a Chinese student at Chung Hua in 1965, She later came to England to study nursing and married an Englishman. They now live in Doncaster East, a Melbourne suburb which seemed identical to the set of 'Neighbours'. In two days we experienced such a wealth of Aussie charm. How I would like to laugh again with Bet about bathing in Lay Eng's marble bathroom. We used too much bath solution, turned on the jacuzzi spa system, and filled the bathroom with bubbles. We tried to push them out through a window but the marble was now as lethal as any ice rink. We slithered about naked and giggled. Heaven knows what our hosts thought we were doing. We panned for gold at Sovereign Hill and recognised a Cornish shovel! We cuddled koalas at Healsville, ate spare ribs in a spare rib restaurant, and rode the trams, Not bad for two days! I wonder what images are now passing through Bet's mind. I cannot tell. Her closed eyes remain closed and her face still. There are no wrinkles on her face. She has never used make up. Until these last few months no one ever believed that she was 70!

"We liked New Zealand didn't we? Do you remember how we thought that we would like to live in The Bay of Islands? We didn't want to live anywhere near Rotarua though did we?" I struggle to

272

keep going. We had loved New Zealand – but then we had been happy together wherever we had been.

For some unknown reason I am continuing to recount our 'World Trip'.

"Do you remember those lovely blueberry muffins we ate in the museum full of chamber pots? Do you remember your birthday – driving back to Auckland in Tom's automatic car and being so relieved that we hadn't pranged it! And Tom had cooked us steak and opened a bottle of champagne!"

Perhaps I am imagining but I sense that she held my hand a little tighter. She is listening. I hope she is able to recall the happiness we shared.

"And I know you remember our two days in Sydney. The walk in the Blue Mountains was just your cup of tea – and you had twinings and I had Fosters!" Strange how the mind can recall such detail and can have simply no recollection of so many broader strokes. Bet doesn't laugh. Why am I doing this?

"And then onto Hong Kong! Your lovely Jackie Tam waiting for us!"

I sense that Bet is upset now. I have pushed too far. Jackie is so much one of our family and I know how much Bet would love her to be here. That little twelve year old that Bet brought back to live with us in Scarborough is now lecturing in one of Hong Kong's universities. Her caring husband CM has a responsible job in the MTR (Mass Transit Railway) where reliability is measured to the nearest second. Hong Kong was an amazing experience and Jackie and CM took us on a generosity-packed whirlwind of infinite escalators, super speed elevators, sterile and litter-free underground space ships, romantic ferries and neon dreams. Jackie had prepared her JT Tours itinerary and was determined that we would feel totally pampered. Her love and respect for Bet was so tangible.

Whilst in Hong Kong we had decided that we should take the opportunity to visit China and we booked ourselves onto a four-day 'tour'. We began, just round the corner, in Macau. We were part of a small group of a dozen or so 'tourists – with our Chinese Guide and driver – in a small bus. There were six Americans, a couple from France, an Australian, a Malaysian, a Canadian, and another couple from Britain. An interesting and significant mix! Our guide Fang kept careful control of our movements and also our passports. We visited a school, a farm, a market, a silk factory and a plethora of pagodas and birthplaces! For the first time on our trip we had to accept that we were tourists and we collected small pieces of intricate work – a beautifully crafted piece of sandalwood, intricate paper silhouettes, and carved jade which Bet felt held healing powers. One night we stayed in the White Swan in Guangzhou – the place which boasted that our Queen had stayed there a year previously. I wonder if she escaped out in the evening as we had done. The world beyond the hotel compound was not easy. It was sweltering in an oriental Dickensian under-world and we were soon surrounded by beggars. We had taken nothing of value with us which we found reassuring to some small degree. It was a shocking reminder that we were the fortunate ones.

As we drove northwards the next day it seemed as though the roads were being built before us as we travelled, slowly, in a traffic jam of government lorries and thousands of bicycles. The Americans now began to become more vociferous as they 'demanded' more haste. Eventually the poor driver felt obliged to try to avoid the jam by taking to the pavement. Within seconds police had surrounded the bus. The driver's licence was confiscated and the Americans had to be silenced by the rest of us as they discussed the possibility of bribing the police! Eventually we reached our destination – the Seven Star Crags in Zhaoqing. This was a beautiful spot, peaceful and a welcome contrast from the stifling smog of the Chinese cities.

The plan for our final day seemed pretty straightforward. We were to drive back down to Guangzhou, have lunch with some shopping, collect our passports and take the train back to Hong Kong. At this point it all went haywire – and Bet and I loved it! The bus coughed and spluttered and came to a halt just half a mile into our journey. The Americans soon became agitated. It seems that they had planes to catch and important tasks to fulfil back in the States. They demanded that Fang telephoned for a replacement. Poor Fang had no phone – and there were no telephones within sight. The Americans became louder. They would have to be rescued. The rest of us smiled. Our Malaysian friend was a mechanic and offered to take a look in the engine which happened to be under the floor. With the help of a spanner, which he held in place whilst lying under the seats, we lurched forward for a few more miles. Diesel fumes filled the vehicle but it seemed a small price to pay for movement. We were way out in the rural 'sticks' but we rumbled into a village square and came to a halt. Our Malaysian hero pulled himself out of the oily depths and declared he could do no more. Villagers came out and conversations took place. We climbed out of the stinking bus, into the even more intense heat of the late morning sun, and looked in vain for shade. The Americans were now furious and threatened Fang with legal action. Poor Fang. He didn't know what to do. He decided that he would flag down a lorry and go to the nearest town where the tourist company had an office and might have a replacement bus. Off he went – and our passports with him!

The village elders, cigarettes in their mouths, crawled under the bus and began to hammer. We moved a little further away! In half an hour the engine had been beaten back into life. Now our poor driver had to endure the tirade of American 'supremacy' as the angry section of our group instructed him to follow Fang! We climbed back on board and reached the town only to find that the tourist office was closed and there was no sign of Fang. The Americans were not prepared to give up! They could wait for no one! We set off for Guangzhou. About ten miles from the city the engine died once again. Our Malaysian hero took hold of the spanner once more and we jerked our way forward. It seemed without any warning that the padi fields had been replaced by a six lane motorway. The engine gave one final cough and we came to a standstill. Our driver dashed out into the middle of the roadways and flagged down the passing traffic. There were two empty taxis and an overcrowded local bus. The Americans physically pushed us all away as they dashed for the taxis and drove off. Our driver spoke to the local bus driver and some agreement was made. The rest of us were placed onto the bus and although already full, the passengers made room for us and even offered us seats. They stared at us of course but responded well to our smiles. We had no idea where we were heading. Eventually the bus stopped and they gestured that we should now get off. We were in the city square, just outside the railway station. The bus had left its designated route in order to take us to the station – with the full agreement of the passengers. There was no charge. They all waved as they returned to their journey. Now we were seeing the real China! At that moment, miraculously, Fang appeared with our passports and rail tickets. Our train would leave in 15 minutes. Where were the Americans? Then two taxis pulled onto the station forecourt and the Americans got out after being charged a local fortune and having been driven all around the city. Yes – the real China!

Not all our travels had been quite so exotic but we did always try to tackle them with a sense of fun. We took the children on trips to the Greek Islands and we joined friends in a Majorcan Villa, and we made full use of Golden Rail Holidays! When it was just two of us Bet and I would often take off in impromptu directions. Once we just picked up the address book and decided to work our way round the 'Christmas card list' and just surprise our friends! We pretended to have toothache as we reached our friend Andrew (a dentist) in Hitchin; we feigned legal problems outside Robert's solicitor's office in Scarborough; we caught Hilda Briggs (my ex Head) mid breakfast – and totally surprised (or horrified) so many other friends. Of course everyone was polite about our invasion – and I think everyone was genuinely pleased! We interspersed our foray with nights in hotels – the places we had never stayed in but always admired. We stayed a night in The Holbeck Hall Hotel just days before it slid down the Scarborough cliffs and into the sea. And we even returned to Speech House and looked again for the red carpet!

One Summer, the girls went off to Scarborough for a catch up with their old friends. Bet and I set about decorating their vacated bedrooms. It was a dismal morning and raining. We looked at each other, packed our toothbrushes and a spare pair of pants each into a plastic bag, and climbed into the car. At the A30 we looked to the right and to the left. It seemed brighter towards the right and so we drove westwards. At each junction we aimed towards the light and eventually we were driving into Penzance. As we were passing the heliport the sun came out and so I pulled into the car park. We grabbed our plastic bag and asked if we could buy a ticket to the Isles of Scilly. This would be a new experience for us – and certainly on our 'to do' list. They could fly us out but only if we had accommodation booked. They gave us a list of hotels and directed us to a phone. I started at the top of the list and was in luck. There was a double room available. Within half an hour we were on a noisy helicopter with the islands stretching below us. We arrived in the tiny arrivals area to hear our names being 'paged'. There before us was a chauffeur, bedecked in full regalia.

"Your luggage sir?"

We handed over our plastic bag! And we had the most amazing four days – despite having to buy ourselves a little more clothing!

We have had such lovely adventures. I do so wish that I could share them again with Bet. She is a little restless. It seems cruel somehow to be even thinking of better times. It is selfish of me to dwell on my memories. I pick up her "Childhood Memories" and ask her if she would like me to read them again. She does. Her eyes remained close but as I read to her I know that she is back on the farm.

She is back with 'her friend Walter'.

'Kaki Panjang'

Monday 23rd November 2015

I am alone again today. I am feeling strangely anxious, and am almost reluctant to press the silver button to open the doors. I know Bet is near to death …

As I always do, when courage begins to fail me, I reassure myself, by going back in my mind to August 1965. After three days 'orientation' in Kuching, the small Dakota, with the innocent, gangly, twenty one year old me on board, landed on the short runway of Sibu Airport. Through the haze of the bright tropical sun I could see a group of three people – my reception committee. There was one woman, Madam Leong who was to translate and introduce me to my Headmaster, Mr Fu and to Mr Chew, the Discipline Master. Neither of the men spoke any English and I suddenly felt very alone and ill – prepared. The Chinese language is very tonal and can be quite strident. There was much earnest discussion as I was whisked into a taxi and we drove the few miles to see Chung Hua School along Lanang Road. This was to be my home for a year. We soon left the concrete and metal of the town. The glaring tarmac of the road drew a clear boundary between the old and the new. On one side was the wide river. To my left, beyond the deep monsoon drainage ditch, were small kampongs – groups of small wooden houses built up on stilts to keep them above the frequent flooding. There were pathways, worn by bare feet and bicycle tyres, disappearing through the palm trees and into the edge of the rain forest oozing with tropical humidity and distinctive sounds. Groups of semi-naked children played on wooden bridges and stared as our taxi passed by. Above all I remember the warmth and the scents. I could never describe them other than through words like 'heavy' and 'spiced', but they are, for me, so much part of the Far East.

There was plenty of urgent conversation, but non of it seemed to be directed at me. The oriental faces would react with a faint smile if my eyes met theirs – but otherwise I seemed to be a disappointment to them. We arrived at the school, and although I had written to them months earlier, I had received no information. I was surprised by the fact that the buildings were all very new. The compound was built at the furthest edge of the town's development. Lanang Road came to an end beyond the school gate. Beyond were rubber plantations and then stretching as far as I could see them were low, jungle clad hills. There were four blocks. The first housed the staff room. Then three each had four classrooms. There was a large concreted area which provided basketball pitches. At the far end was an assembly hall as yet hardly used! There were no students or teachers . There was no one apart from Awi , the Malay teenager who, I later discovered, was the staff room 'servant'. He proved to be a great friend and support. I seemed to have arrived on a holiday.

Madam Leong turned from earnest discussion to explain that Mr Fu didn't expect me to begin my teaching until Monday – giving me three days to find somewhere to live. I found myself almost on the edge of tears.

"But VSO expect you to have found me somewhere to live," I found myself almost blubbering. " It is in my contract. You provide accommodation and a basic salary!" It all sounded so pathetic as I stood in the blazing sun waving my arms around like a demented windmill. I had to stop myself from screaming for my mum!

There was much further discussion and at times it sounded as though it was reaching the stage of verbal battle. The taxi was still there and Madam Leong explained that she would take me to see a friend, an Australian, who might have a spare bed. He was a pleasant enough guy but he was a missionary and this aspect worried me. His home was fairly primitive and it was obvious that, although I could have stayed with him, there really wasn't enough room. I decided that I would try to find somewhere myself and Madame Leong dropped me and my bag in the centre of Sibu. I sat at a typical Chinese 'coffee shop' and suddenly wanted to go home! Part of that yearning also included Bet and the farm! I missed them all – and for a few minutes I thought I had made a terrible mistake.

At my lowest moment a bright eyed, smiling young Chinese man came over and politely asked if I was from England. He wanted to know if I had met the Queen and if I knew The Beatles for he was going to study in London in a week's time and was hopeful that I could arrange introductions! We spent an hour or so with me answering his torrent of searching questions about life 'back home' but he also was interested in me and what I was doing in Sarawak. He offered to help me find somewhere to live. He gathered up my bag and led me along the main roadways. We would climb stair wells and knock on doors. There would be a look of shock cross the faces as my guide obviously asked if they had any rooms to spare. It seemed to be that I was a foreigner and as such, not welcome. Back home we had known racial tensions and the 'colour bar' was tarnishing places like Birmingham. Was this what was happening here? Only much later did I discover that the only British people they had known were the Raj – Rajah Brooke and his family, and Government officials. An ordinary Chinese family home would have been far too basic for any one of such status to visit, never mind live in! When we came to the rooms rented by the Lau family there was a far more positive response. The Mother, Mrs Lau, was bringing up her two children alone as, I later came to understand, Mr Lau had taken wife number two and spent most of his time elsewhere. Lau Yong was about nine years old and Lau Ching, his little sister, was five. Mother realised that I could not only help her financially, but she recognised the value of having an English teacher as part of her family. There was a spare room. We could buy a bed and a table and chair from the shop across the road – Ramin Way. All suddenly seemed to be more positive. By the time my young 'guide' left me the whole neighbourhood seemed to have gathered to stare at my white skin. I desperately needed a wee! My drama skills – mime in particular – came into play and Mother seemed to understand. She led me down the corridor, all her friends and neighbours following her, down into the kitchen area. There were two adjacent cubicles. I was pushed into the furthest one and saw in front of me the typical Asian toilet, the basic hole in the floor, but this one seemed very civilised with a flush tank above. By now the crowd resembled an enthusiastic theatre audience and I found myself almost waving and bowing to them as I closed the door. Achh!! Something jumped onto my shoulder. I looked down and stared into the glistening eyes of a gigantic rat! I was horrified and struck it violently. It fell down into the toilet hole and struggled to get itself out. I reached up for the chain and tugged in desperation. The cacophony of excitement became even louder and several hands seemed to be banging on the door. I opened to the sea of voices.

"No! No!" I had set the tone. Like a game a charades, with about twenty people playing simultaneously, I had to work out that the plumbing, although it looked the part, had never been coupled up. To flush the loo one had to take the bucket and go into the next cubicle. This was the shower room but again although this looked efficient, it was basically a large tub, a tap and a big ladle! With help from the crowd we did manage to flush the rat away and I presume I eventually managed to empty my bladder.

That night I sat on my new bed, clutching my 'Dutch Widow', and wrote my first entry into my diary. I had to reflect on the day. It had not been easy but somehow I had survived. I didn't sleep well for it was hot and humid. I had windows wide open and the lights of Ramin Way were glaring in stark contrast to the black sky beyond. I often got up and looked out onto the street below. The shop houses stayed open for a long time and I could hear the sound of the clattering of marjong pieces as old men chattered loudly towards midnight. It is impossible to whisper in Chinese! Open shops, the sounds of Chinese. How ironic! This was the most urban scene I had ever inhabited and yet it was in the middle of Borneo, 100 miles inland and yet only 10 feet above sea level. From my window I could see a petrol station – and yet there were few cars. There were few roads, just one going out to the air strip and another, the 'Oya Road" proudly stretched 20 miles out to a new agricultural station. There were no road links to any other town and entry to Sibu was by air or by boat. In my wallet, rapidly becoming empty of the few ringits I had brought with me, I had a photo of Bet. – my best friend. I knew now that I had left behind someone with whom I wanted to share my life. There was a danger that I was over reacting. This could certainly be a rebound situation brought on by a severe bout of home-sickness. I tried to analyse the situation but my thoughts were often disturbed by the scuttling of rats as they traversed the top of my walls (the partitions had open ventilation at the top) as they made their way through to the kitchen for their nightly feast alongside the cockroaches – not that I fully appreciated this accepted routine on that first night. It was just another shattering experience that I had to face!

As often happens in my life, by the morning I had made a decision. It was surely acceptable to marry ones best friend! I knew Bet had other 'boy friends' and that had been a mutually acceptable way we had lived our lives but I really felt that we belonged together. The farm, her lovely dad, her quirky mum – they seemed so much a part of me – or what I wanted to be. The next day, armed with Lau Yong's assistance and determination to speak English, I made it to the post office and posted Bet a letter. I explained how I felt as I had driven away from the farm a week previously – and I asked her if she would marry me. The anxiety of the wait for her reply was background now to an ongoing marathon of hurdles. Thankfully I had a new family and Yong and Ching had named me "Kaki Panjang" – which in Malay means 'long legs'!

I needed a bicycle. Every one it seemed had a bicycle. I borrowed one from a friend of my new family and cycled out the three miles along Lanang Road to Chung Hua. The school was now in session and there were hundreds of cycles parked in the front area. Awi was there to greet me – his beaming smile reassuring. Madam Leong listened to my saga, which I proudly pronounced, and this started a serious debate which involved entering Mr Fu's Office. This opened up onto the senior management area which Madam Leong shared with Mr Chew (who always held a fan and used it to good effect in his task of Discipline Master) and a rather wise looking Mr Moo who seemed to be responsible for the timetable. This office in turn opened up onto the staff room. Each teacher had a desk facing right through to the Head's Office – the idea being that Mr Foo could watch to see that all his staff were marking or preparing lessons. There was never any idle chatter! I was assured that I would be reimbursed for the cost of the bed, bicycle and that the school would pay Madam Lau the monthly rent. There was no mention of when that would be and a serious cash flow problem loomed!

I was then introduced to some of the staff. They were all Chinese with the exception of two Indian teachers – Mr Phillips (pronounced Pillips!), who was the Head of English, and Mr Abrahams who taught Science. It was immediately obvious that only a minority of the staff could speak English, or at least had the confidence to try. My desk had a name plate – and my name was written in Chinese characters. Every notice on the board was written in Chinese and there was no English anywhere. This was not the welcome I had expected or been led to believe by VSO. I later came to understand. Three years previously the Government had decreed that English would become the medium for Education throughout the State and therefore all Chinese schools would have to convert to that language for the majority of their lessons. Suddenly a whole group of well educated Chinese teachers were faced with having to learn enough English to be able to teach their subject – or find that they were made to leave their profession. Chung Hua had not asked for a Volunteer from Britain. I had been sent there by the Education Department, concerned by the lack of progress being made by the school. No wonder there was no obvious 'welcome' – no garlands placed on me by dusky maidens that I had initially envisaged way back earlier in the year when I had asked the VSO interviewing panel if they could place me on a Pacific island! No one told me this, until very much later. I just had to fight my way through what seemed a barrage of difficulties.

I negotiated, or at least my little brother Yong did for me, the purchase of a cycle, with the promise of payment later. The colour of my skin and the fact that I was an 'honourable teacher" seemed to have some advantages. I was a novelty item already and it seemed that every one knew that 'kaki panjang' now lived with Family Lau in Ramin Way. I suppose news had filtered through to my new students who must have stared in amazement as I cycled alongside them en route for the 8am start. There was to be an assembly. The classes marched out with military precision and stood in rows before a constructed dais on which senior staff were to be seated. The sun was blazing down and it was already alarmingly hot. There was a primitive sound system and Mr Fu's voice echoed through the surrounding rubber plantation. I had been told that I would be introduced to the school and I had hurriedly prepared. I stepped forward to the microphone. A sea of white and blue before me. Faces staring in anticipation. I had to get this right.

"Nui tah cah chia quor horto …" It seemed right to speak in Chinese and show a willingness to learn their language. After all I was going to expect them to speak to me in English. I anticipated a degree of acknowledgement as I told them of my journey to school by bicycle! There was nothing. Not a glimmer of response. Just hundreds of faces staring at me. I tried again.

"Nui tah cah chia quor horto ..." Again nothing.

And so I spoke in English and got a very rapturous response!

Chinese is a tonal language and without the right inflection the meaning is lost or completely distorted. When I left the school, seventeen months later, I was determined to make amends. I began my fairly long farewell speech in the correct formal way.

"Shiojan, Lau Tzu ..." which translated should mean 'Principal, teachers ...'"

Afterwards I asked my class how I had fared. They were impressed, and told me that I had only made one tonal error. I had apparently got the inflection wrong with my 'Lau Tzu'. So what was the error? What had I called my fellow members of staff? I had apparently called them 'rats'. A little knowledge eh?

I loved my classes. They were so responsive. From now on, whatever I was doing, I felt that there would be someone nearby who would help. I discovered that I could buy pineapples from the wayside on my way 'home'; there were lovely street food vendors cooking nasi goring and mee; and there was even a store that imported tins of baked beans! The great boost to my confidence was when I got Bet's letter assuring me that she would love to share her life with me! From then on I could show everyone her photo and tell them that this was the girl whom I would marry! I would never be alone again.

She is lying very still, cocooned in a nest of clean white pillows. I can hear her breathing It is hollow now. It has the echo of death. Her face looks even smoother. I clean her mouth and offer her a sip of water. I am annoyed that the swabs have not yet arrived. Amazon have let me down! She seems at peace and happy that it is just me. Fran and Jennie had made the journey down from Exeter again a couple of days ago but Bet had not wanted to sing this time.

I take out my note book. Each day now I spend a few moments reading out simple messages I want her to hear. I can read them – but I am not sure if I could say them otherwise. I would cry. As it is, by focusing on the actually written words, I am able to hopefully convey something of my love. How I regret not having told her these things every day of our lives.

"I have always loved you. There has never been anyone else. You must know that."

"Do you know how much you supported me when I first went to Sarawak? I have never told you until now. I couldn't have achieved what I did without you being at home waiting for me"

Not that I was to realise just what I had achieved until five years ago. In 2011 I received an email asking if I would mind if some of my Sarawak students made contact. I was delighted of course. There was to be a reunion, 45 years on, of my two favourite classes 3a and 3b. Bet and I were invited, as guests, to attend. We immediately booked flights out to Kuching for there we were to be hosted by the 'Reunion Committee' and as guests we would be placed into hotels, flown to Sibu and then treated to a visit to Mulu and the National Park. What an experience that proved to be. In Kuching, at the airport, we were met by Mee Seng and his charming wife Cynthia who whisked us off to the luxurious Pulman Hotel where they had a surprise arranged. They had traced my little 'brother' Yong (who I hadn't seen since he hurriedly left England in 1974) and my even smaller 'sister' Ching! By sheer coincidence Ching and Cynthia were really close friends but despite all the planning it had dawned on neither of them that they were to meet up with 'Kaki Panjang'. Yong had become a very successful banker and business man and now lived in Kuala Lumpur. He and his wife had flown over to meet us. That was just the beginning of emotional meetings. Celebration after celebration – typical Chinese banquets. Story after story, life after life, and all had a common thread. They all wanted to thank me for changing their lives. They all explained how I had opened their eyes to a new way of thinking about the world. I had seemed as a breath of cool fresh air as I burst into their classrooms, arms waving, with a verbosity and enthusiasm that was such a startling contrast to the classical Chinese system. I was not 'god' – I was not the fountain of all knowledge – I was not the task master – just an ordinary young person from the other side of the world who tried to give them confidence and to be themselves. I did push boundaries I know. Traditionally there was never 'education' outside the classroom but I, against the wishes of Mr Fu apparently (but as I could never understand what he said I had decided sometimes it was worth the risk!) took them on adventures. One weekend we hired a launch and went down the Kut canal to the seaside. The spluttering and shrieking which took place as they entered the sea was initially worrying. I had just neglected to tell them that sea water was salty and not good to drink!

I took my classes out to the Agricultural Station along the Oya Road, where VSO had placed a lovely young man, Andrew Burgess. My students relished this practical application of science and it made a lasting impression on many. Sadly Andrew died a few weeks after our visit. His land rover hit a rut on the rough roadway, turned over, and Andrew didn't survive. I was to visit his grave in 2011 – a very moving experience. A reminder, perhaps, of just how challenging VSO had been for us all back in 1965/66.

My final 'school trip' was, at that time, very ambitious indeed. Initially I had planned to take a group of students over the South China Sea and onto mainland Malaya. We were planning to stay at schools and challenge them to basketball games. Sadly there was an outbreak of yellow fever and all deck passage was cancelled. There was no way we could afford to travel in cabins and so I had to reorganise quickly. I decided to take them to the capital city – to Kuching. Non of them had been there before so it could still be a valuable experience. We were able to travel very cheaply on the 'Rejang', an old tub of a boat that plied backwards and forwards at a leisurely pace between Sibu and Kuching, and we found several schools where we could stay and play! As this appeared to be Sarawak's first school trip of such ambitious proportions, I found it easy to arrange visits that would, certainly in today's climate of health and safety, never have otherwise been possible. We went to the prison and toured through the cells, being introduced to the inmates; we went into a 'leper colony' and sat with sad folk who had been banished behind high fences; and we walked through mangrove swamps which probably were home to crocodiles.

Apparently though it was my actual classroom style which had enthused my students so much. Their English lessons had been dull. Instead of the 'Turn to page 12, Exercise 14" (delivered in a very strong Indian accent) I had filled the hour with living language, with description and story, and with fun and laughter. As the 'Geography Teacher' I had been told that the previous year almost all the students had failed the exam as there had been a map of the world on which they had been asked to name cities, rivers and mountain ranges. On the back wall of classroom 3a and 3b I had drawn out three world maps. Each day three students had to remove all the named flags and replace them in the correct place. By the end of the year they all knew every major city, every important river and all the world's natural wonders. When the exam came there was, this year, no world map! I think that experience taught me so much about the limitations of 'exams'! However, when Bet and I were invited to Mee Seng's home, there on the wall was a world map with flags pinned into it. These were the places he had visited! They did all pass their Geography exam despite my teaching!

What was so lovely was that in 2011 it was actually Bet who stole the show. She fitted in so well and my students responded as though they were old friends. She did in fact feel completely at home – but she always did. She had heard my 'jungle stories' so often over the forty five intervening years, She had always supported my narratives – and always laughed with sincerity in the right places. She had always agreed with me when I had made political points. She had grown old with me as I enthused about the generosity of native tribes and now she was here, in Sarawak, with my 'family' and could finally understand.

I have a lovely photograph of Bet, by the roadside with a group of Chinese 'students'. She is relishing slices of durian – the stinking fruit! I hated the smell, the taste and the texture. It was once described as 'eating cold custard whilst sitting in a sewer' but that I thought, was far too tame! The Chinese love it. Now Bet was loving it too! A convert. Something I could never be.

There were things that could never be recaptured. The long houses now have electricity. The head hunters' swords and the baskets of skulls have largely been confined to the cultural museum. The punans are now pathetically re housed in 'villages' courtesy of Government initiatives which tear down their rain forest and replace it with palm oil! Bet understands and shares my sorrow.

Bet knew all about Swee Kee when he popped up before us. She knew how I had encouraged him, as a fifteen year old, onto the stage and how he had loved to act and sing. And now he was standing before us, as animated as ever.

"Oh Mr Peter. How glad I am to see you. I wanted so much to thank you! I went on to study Drama in London and then in New York. All my career I have used your method of direction!"

I looked on puzzled.

"I have taken cake and pop into every rehearsal!"

Bet laughed with me as she always did. She must have heard my 'crocodile story' hundreds of times but never failed to support me. She never failed to laugh at my account of how VSO Colleen Eyton Williams had dressed for dinner on our first night in Sarawak – and how the drunken Irish man had seen her waft by in her long sarong and called after her.

"Here! Pull your drawers up Fifi!"

Colleen has been 'Fifi' ever since. She is still a very close friend and has made the journey from London to visit Bet. A gang of VSO's would get together in the school holidays and travel. I suppose, just so we didn't feel too guilty about 'enjoying ourselves', we would each take one of our students with us. I took Kek Ming when we travelled through Brunei and into Sabah. There we climbed Kinabalu, sleeping in a primitive wooden hut just before the summit. I remember waking in the night to see poor Kek Ming kneeling on the floor and praying to his god. We had forgotten to explain how the temperature would drop. The boy thought his world was ending. We did make the summit by day break but sadly it was shrouded in mist. Probably a good job as I don't really have a good head for heights! Fifi and I travelled up Malaya in the summer of 1966. We know exactly where we were when England won the World Cup! On the edge of the jungle in Malacca watching on a black and white television which had been imported especially for the occasion. The locals were thrilled that England won and threw a party to celebrate. We were the guests of honour. Britain was still held in high regard at that time. Sadly we are no longer as welcome as we were. The world has changed! On that same journey we witnessed the start of the dramatic transformation as Thailand was responding to western money! American soldiers were using Thailand for respite from the Vietnam War. The money they were throwing at locals to 'have a good time' was the beginning of what Thailand has become today – a vast treasure chest of what it feels western society wants! An image I will always carry with me is of an old lady begging on the platform of Bankok Station. I had a ticket back to Singapore but no more money. Fifi, who was returning to Britain, had bought me a great bunch of grapes – and that would be my food for the next two days. The old lady thought I was American and a soldier. She obviously believed that I had money and grabbed hold of me and wouldn't let me go. I had to knock her to the ground. I will never forget. I was heading back to Sarawak, having extended my tour, to finish teaching my examination classes and continue to be a thorn in the senior management team – who never really came to appreciate me! My train ticket got me to Singapore where I managed to hitch a lift with the British Army – who were fighting 'confrontation' over on Borneo. That was always good for I would be given 'rations' of proper sandwiches and even a Kit Kat biscuit!

I eventually did get home –just two days before Christmas. My initial flight out of Sarawak was in a small, light plane – the sort where one had to be weighed before take off. My luggage was too heavy and I had to make a quick decision. My travel bag with my clothes, or the ratan around my neck which held together a native shield, a parang and some Iban carvings. No brainer! And so there I was at 5pm on a freezing damp night on the platform of King's Cross waiting for the train to Doncaster. I had a vest and shorts – and nothing else to wear. But the colourful display round my neck made an impact! And Bet was there to meet me at Doncaster. She gave me her coat!

"Thank you Bet for being with me. Thank you. Thank you"

In 2012 a group of my 'students' took up my invitation to travel to Falmouth for some further geography lessons. Bet was, as always, such a caring host and they loved her. She had shared so much of their lives during our visit the previous year. She had

shown such a compassionate interest in their lives –
and they knew, as everyone did, that Bet's concern
was always genuine.

> *"Thank you Bet! You ate the durian and enjoyed it! Kaki Panjang has always loved you! Please don't forget! I never will!"*

"The Carnival is Over"

Tuesday 24th November 2015 1.30pm

Something is wrong. I sign the visitor's book and I am aware that the Manager is standing by and waiting for me. I follow her into her office.

Bet had passed away just a few minutes earlier. I had not been there. The last part of our journey and she had made it alone.

I had the box of mouth swabs in my bag.

For the carnival is over
We may never meet again…
Written in 1965 by Tom Springfield for The Seekers

One of our favourite songs.

Bet's Farewell

Monday 7th December 2015 Glyn Valley Crematorium 1.30pm

We entered to a Neil Diamond song "Come Dry your Eyes". Neil kept us sewing for many hours in our puppet workshop.

Peter, Joe and Katie had gifts for Bet to take on her journey. Pete sent along an otter puppet. Katie sent Bet's 'Golly' that Bet had owned since she was three years old. Katie kept Bet's Teddy though and promised to look after it. Joe gave Bet one of her crystals – a beautiful round jade ball. He remembered playing with it when he was very young and Bet pointing out that it wasn't a toy!

Katie then joined her mum and Donna as they sang "A Winter's Tale".

Pete read the words of one of the first song's he wrote. "Words Weaving Tapestry" was from "The Inn of Happiness". Of all his lyrics this remained something very special:

The poet looks and he sees beauty
The day was warm
Children were flying their scarlet kites
High against the blue of the skies
Chasing in magic like lovers
Dreaming a land where fortune flies
The poet looks and he sees beauty

Evening cool
The breeze is blowing the lantern's light
High into the spill of the moon
Shadows are dancing on lovers
Knowing that night is coming soon

I look and I see beauty
Your face so clear
Your eyes are shining their living glow
So gentle your skin and so fine
Beauty is written by lovers
Tracing their words on forest pine

Words weaving tapestry, butterfly soft,
Spinning silk in the clouds, delicate sound
Whispering "Woe ai nee" I love you.

Fran also wrote a poem which Jennie read so beautifully. It follows. As Bet's friends left the chapel Joe gave each one a cherry liquor sweet, which he explained had, surprisingly, become Bet's favourite. Katie gave everybody a daffodil which out friend Paul had sent along – the first of Bet's best-loved spring flowers.

Nothing Lost

Though all seemed lost
in those last hours,
to see you gasping on the shore of

life;
And more, before
in lashing out
to where Love lay, as if
the past was just
a wind-swept tide at play.
No. Not this
will greet the dawning day;
but partnership across
a strand of years
and banks of kindness
built in harmony.
each random act of violence
to remind how far
your boat has come adrift
under your darkened star.
It is later now.
We are no longer by those tempests tossed
for it was but a borderline you crossed.
Nothing sweet in those last times achieved
but in the drift of oceans
nothing lost.

Francis Hallam December 2015

Reflections:

Monday 19th September 2016
Cologne Cathedral

I find myself, notebook in hand, sitting here in awe. How many thousands of souls have worked here, their sweat and tears ingrained into the stone? Did each one imagine a life beyond? Not for me. Heaven would be far too cluttered – a turmoil of emotional ties. I will settle for what I have, for what I have lost, and for what is still to come. Bet is no longer. She has no more suffering – no more tears. And yet here, in this masterpiece of Gothic architecture I am certain I can hear the echoes of the past. Listen hard and I can hear Bet's laughter and I can remember her joy.

My scribble is becoming blurred. My eyes are watering again! I am not sure of all this sadness. It is good that I miss Bet so very much but I am struggling to find reasons why I must 'get on' with my life when at times I feel so hopelessly lost. I have moved into my 'granddad cave' – a lovely conversion to part of Sam and Ian's house – and everyone, including grandchildren Joe and Katie seem at ease with this. I have created a rose garden for Bet, with the old-fashioned fragrant varieties that she loved. I cook tea most evenings and do the daily shopping – the 'au pair' in the family's busy life. Not that I am much use to them today sitting miles away in a cathedral. Maybe this is where I 'sort myself out', shake myself up, and somehow move forward.

I have travelled a few times over the past months. I joined Fran and Jennie at the end of their Camino trail and then spent a week with Fifi and her husband Hugh in Mirapoix. Now I am travelling across Germany alone. It is as though I have to break through this barrier. Around me hundreds of people move through this place and I watch them as their eyes cover the vast canopies of time. I imagine what Bet and I would say to each other. There would be just the odd incidental words – but it is those that I miss so much. In the past they would have seemed almost insignificant, vacuous even, yet now I realise too late just how important they were for it is through those close to us that we can reach an understanding of ourselves.

I have completed my book and now I must decide where to go with it.

It has been therapeutic – I am sure. It has enabled me to focus on Bet before the illness contorted her body and her mind. In a sense, I am now able to reflect on her illness and talk and think about it in a more dispassionate way. After all, it is now a story. What kind of story have I written? Friends, reading the initial draft, have mixed opinions. Some feel that I have distorted the main focus, and therefore its value, by writing too much about myself and my own career. An interesting point. I think this reflects something about me as a 'carer'. For two years I had devoted my existence almost entirely to trying to meet Bet's needs.

With her form of dementia she was unable to offer any form of thanks – and, as so often is the case, inflicted torrents of physical and verbal abuse. Those of you who are caring now for a loved one will recognise the need for someone, somehow, to help you rebuild your own self-esteem. You will feel drained – not just of physical and emotional energy, but of your own personality and your own sense of worth. My writing has reflected my own search for self-reassurance. Each one of us, in this situation, needs to find support – through friends, family or from one's own inner resources. Sadly society, as a whole, is in danger of allowing 'caring' to become undervalued. We do so at our peril.

I pause now from my notes and look around. How many thousands of people move across these stone floors each day? Each is a unique individual; each needing to feel wanted and loved. We don't always support those we love as much as they need. We often assume that all is well, for we can never hope to fully understand the complexities of the human mind. If we could recognise sooner that the 'reality' within the one we love has altered, then perhaps we would not react in ways that alienate rather than support. How Bet must have been saddened and disturbed by my reactions in those early days of her dementia. She saw the person she loved – her best friend for over fifty years – now frowning, getting angry, no longer the easy going smiling soul – but tense, agitated and completely changed. Bet's reality was as it was. My constant attempts to 'correct' her, through 'my logic', were invalid and counter-productive. I inadvertently was increasing her sense of frustration – as if her body wasn't suffering enough. I have seen some really wonderful care of people with dementia – where the individual's 'reality' is respected as far as possible. Maybe we all need to be more sensitive to the intricacies of the human mind. Mental illness is so little understood – and relevant research so grossly under funded.

The sun streams through the stained glass. It is deflected, altered no doubt, but the warmth is still there. I can feel it and appreciate it. More than that, I can wonder at its joy. Such energy influences everything. I can pick out any single individual from the swirling mass of humanity around me and 'life' is there – energy again. Such are the forces, the dreams, the ideals, the fears the prejudices, the horrors and the loves. Even when close to someone we can only understand so little of their existence. And yet some elements of personality are so obvious and unquestionable and can never be denied. I must remember that there wasn't even a 'tickle' of malice within Bet before the illness relentlessly destroyed her. I will take with me the essence of her love, her smile, her ability not to judge and to see goodness in all those she met. I must keep her love safe and something of her dreams alive. I will never forget. I will try to accept that during the past few years it was illness that distorted everything. As Fran says in his poem:

Nothing sweet in those last times achieved
but in the drift of oceans
nothing lost.

Those who built this cathedral left something behind. I think each one of us will leave something of ourselves – we may not see it, but, like the warmth from the sun, it could still be good.

I'll put my notebook away now and carry on my journey. I am no longer alone. I realise now that Bet will always be with me. This is our book. We have written it together. And as for the dilemma as to where it will slot onto the library shelves – our friend Joan tells me there is no doubt.

"It is a love story!" she claims.

We can't argue with that!